STUDIES IN HISTORY AND ARCHAEOLOGY

General Editor
F. T. WAINWRIGHT

ROMAN AND NATIVE IN NORTH BRITAIN

ROMAN AND NATIVE in NORTH BRITAIN

Edited by

I. A. RICHMOND

NELSON
1958

THOMAS NELSON AND SONS LTD
Parkside Works Edinburgh 9
36 Park Street London W1
312 Flinders Street Melbourne C1
302–304 Barclays Bank Building
Commissioner and Kruis Streets
Johannesburg

THOMAS NELSON AND SONS (CANADA) LTD
91–93 Wellington Street West Toronto 1

THOMAS NELSON AND SONS
19 East 47th Street New York 17

SOCIÉTÉ FRANÇAISE D'EDITIONS NELSON
97 rue Monge Paris 5

EDITOR'S PREFACE

THE subjects considered in this volume have been tackled, as readers will appreciate, from widely differing points of view. Since, however, in ancient times both the initiative in policy and the means of recording it in literature or epigraphy lay with Rome, it will not be surprising if the colouring of the picture is Roman. The historian will observe that the point which emerges most clearly is the cardinal fact that the interaction of Roman and native produced and consolidated a political and economic pattern which formed the background of the cultural pattern of Scotland in later ages, and that this was probably the first occasion upon which such a ground could be prepared. The impact of Rome upon these islands is often elusive of definition, and her relations with Scotland are frequently dismissed as episodic and ephemeral. The effect of these studies is to show that, while the cultural side of the relationship was never sufficiently developed to bear fruit, its political side linked Scotland this side of the Mounth with the south in perpetuity. So was created the shape of things to come.

The evidence upon which these conclusions are based is not the normal stuff of history. Querns and coins or pottery and dress-fasteners are archaeologists' material. But to the proto-history of the lands beyond the Roman Empire it is archaeological evidence which has most to contribute, and in Scotland this is the first occasion upon which it has been used in broad outline to amplify the more conventional sources for a general survey.

In arranging the material the editor's task has been light, thanks to the finished form in which the contributions reached him.

I. A. R.

March 1958

CONTENTS

ACKNOWLEDGMENTS

THANKS are due and are hereby tendered to the following for permission to reproduce prints :

The Keeper, The National Museum of Antiquities, Edinburgh (Plate 5, above ; Plate 6, below right) ; Robert Adam Esq. (Plate 5, below) ; The Director of the National Museum of Wales (Plate 6, above) ; Glasgow University Court (Plate 6, below left) ; Carlisle Public Library Committee (Plate 7, above) ; J. P. Gillam Esq. (Plate 7, below) ; The Society of Antiquaries of Newcastle upon Tyne (Plate 8).

Plates 1–4 are reproduced from *Die Reliefs der Traians-säule* by C. Cichorius, Berlin 1896–1900.

LIST OF ILLUSTRATIONS

Plates (between pages 86 and 87)

Maps

In Text

Chapter I

NATIVE ECONOMIES AND THE ROMAN OCCUPATION OF NORTH BRITAIN

I

THE relationship between Roman and Briton during the earlier centuries of the Christian era can be considered from more than one point of view. The first, the political reaction of tribes and individuals to the events leading up to and during the occupation, can be deduced in part from literary sources and, in lesser degree and by inference, from the evidence of archaeology : this, the province of the historian, has been discussed on numerous occasions. The impact of Mediterranean art, as exemplified by Roman provincial styles, upon the non-representational traditions of the Celtic world, has again been the subject of comment and analysis. But one aspect, of crucial importance to the invading military forces, has not received the attention which is its due. To what degree was there divergence between the economic bases of the Early-Iron-Age population of Britain and those of the classical world brought in by the Romans ? How far, in the production of essential foodstuffs, could the native resources provide for an army accustomed in large part to live off the land during its campaigns ? Any answers to such questions must be based largely upon archaeological evidence, and it is my purpose here to examine this problem in relation to the Roman advance into, and occupation of, North Britain.

The destruction of the endearing myth of the naked, woad-bedaubed savage waving his flint-headed axe at the resolute Romans on some Kentish beach has, and with justice, been noted as something of an achievement in British archaeology and its popularisation. In his place there has been portrayed the farmer in timber-built steading or hamlet, or stone-walled broch and wheel-house ; the craftsman and artist in pottery and enamel-work, armourer and blacksmith, fort-builder and chariot-wright. Nor were many of these skills innovations, but could be seen stretching back through the Bronze Age to the first farming communities of Neolithic colonists at the very beginning of the second millennium B.C. : the Early Iron Age took its place alongside comparable technological stages elsewhere in the Old World, including the shores of the Mediterranean. Indeed, in the first flush of enthusiasm for the rehabilitation of the immediately pre-Roman Briton the phrases ' Iron-Age Hill-Towns ' and even ' City ' or ' Metropolis ' were used, conveying an impression that the state of civilisation encountered by the Romans in this island, though sensibly more barbarian than their own, differed in degree rather than in kind.

The circumstances briefly indicated above unconsciously created a climate of thought in which the Early Iron Age was regarded as representing the culmination of a long process of agricultural development in Britain, more or less coincident with the extensive use of the traction-plough for the first time, and spread throughout the island. In Scotland, for instance, Childe saw evidence for ' indirectly intensified agriculture and an increased reliance on cereal foods . . . among all societies ' at this time,[1] no less than on the Wessex and Sussex downs, and it has been generally felt, if not specifically expressed, that Early-Iron-Age Britain was as a whole to be considered as a land of relatively intense grain-growing.[2]

Two additional factors contributed to this view. In the first place, while an antithetical relationship between farming and hunter-fisher communities was clearly perceptible in the early second millennium B.C. in northern Europe, it was generally assumed that some form of stable agricultural economy had become established over the whole area by the Late Bronze

[1] V. G. Childe, *Scotland before the Scots* (1946), 82

[2] ' Indeed this system of farming continued among the various Iron-Age groups all over England until and into the period of Roman occupation,' S. Piggott, *British Prehistory* (1949), 153–4.

Age at least. In the Early Bronze Age, it is true, some sort of pastoral nomadism had been inferred for certain communities by some archaeologists, though the evidence was rather indirect.[1] But on the whole a continuous development of agricultural techniques from the Neolithic onwards, accelerated by innovations in the Late Bronze Age and Early Iron Age, was visualised as having taken place all over Britain.[2]

The second factor arose from the accidental concentration of archaeological field-work and excavation on Early-Iron-Age sites within the southern English chalk downland for a couple of decades from the time of Crawford's initial recognition of prehistoric field systems there in the 1920s. The excavations of hill-forts in Sussex by Curwen, in Hampshire by Hawkes and in Dorset by Wheeler, and above all the re-assessment of older finds made possible by Bersu's excavation of the farmstead at Little Woodbury in Wiltshire, combined to give a picture of such conviction that it was unconsciously adopted as a norm for Britain as a whole. The economy of the Wessex and Sussex Iron Age was assumed to be typical of the less well-explored regions lying outside its territory: a pattern of stable farming communities growing cereal crops with a well-ordered field-system, accompanied by stock-breeding.

II

It is convenient to begin our critical examination of this position with a brief analysis of the economy of the Wessex-Sussex Iron-Age settlements, or what we may conveniently call the *Woodbury Type* of economy.[3] This is marked by settlement units of single farmstead, or *Einzelhof*, type rather than villages; by stock-breeding, but especially by grain-growing on fields tilled with a traction-plough and laid out in relatively orderly fashion; by the storage of the consumption-

[1] As for instance C. F. C. and J. Hawkes, *Prehistoric Britain* (1947), 55

[2] Cf. E. C. Curwen, *PPS* IV (1938), 27–51, with a 'Pastoral Stage' followed by a 'Stage of Settled Villages' in Britain

[3] G. Bersu, *PPS* VI (1940), 30–111; J. W. Brailsford, ibid. XIV (1948), 1–23, XV (1949), 156–68; C. F. C. Hawkes, *Arch. J.* CIV (1947), 27–81

harvest of grain in pits ; by the practice of parching or roasting the grain before storage ; and by the use, in the farmyards, of structures supported upon posts, which can be interpreted as granaries and drying-racks. The farms may be undefended, or enclosed by a palisade, or by banks and ditches ; they may stand in the open, or be contrived within the defences of hill-forts. As we shall see, elements in this economy go back to the eighth century B.C. or even earlier, but in its characteristic Iron-Age form we know it from the late fifth century B.C. to the time of the Roman Conquest. In terms of the subdivisions of the British Iron Age it is related to the A group rather than to B and C, a point touched on again below.

The existence of a circular timber-built house within a farmyard was demonstrated at Little Woodbury and can be inferred on sites excavated earlier, in which post-holes were not recognised or not sought for (e.g. Woodcuts and Rotherley). The status of settlements within the area of hill-forts, as at Maiden Castle in Dorset or the Caburn in Sussex, is obscure, and we may here be dealing with larger units than the family and dependents totalling perhaps fifteen to twenty persons, deduced from the Woodbury, Woodcuts and Rotherley evidence.[1] The farmstead type, however, can with confidence be seen to have its origins in the Late Bronze Age of both Sussex (Plumpton Plain, New Barn Down) and Wiltshire (Thorny Down).

In the Sussex Late-Bronze-Age sites just mentioned, a direct relationship could be established between the farmsteads and an immediately adjacent series of squarish fields, and, while a similar close association has not been established in bulk for the Early Iron Age or the Romano-British period, the evidence is sufficient to justify the belief that the Woodbury type settlements were in fact closely connected with ploughed lands of the so-called ' Celtic Field ' pattern. The problems of such field-systems are by no means easy of resolution, and classification by field-work alone is fraught

[1] C. F. C. Hawkes, op. cit. 79

with difficulties and may give misleading results if incautiously applied.[1] We shall turn to this point again when considering the distribution of such field-systems in time and space.

Perhaps the most easily identifiable feature of the Woodbury economy is the use of storage pits, which, as 'pit-dwellings,' have had a long and misleading history in British archaeology. Bersu's convincing interpretation of the Woodbury evidence set the whole matter in a new light, consonant with archaeology, analogy and literary evidence alike.[2] Evidence from such Late-Bronze-Age sites as that at Minnis Bay, Birchington,[3] suggests that, like the field-type and the homestead unit, pit-storage may too have its roots in cultures earlier than the Iron Age in this country, and they are certainly found on the earliest sites of Iron Age A so far known, at Fengate and at Scarborough. The same types of storage pits were used by people of both the A and B groups of the British Iron Age, but Belgic (Iron Age C) farming practice seems not on the whole to have used pit-storage in the same manner: on some sites, however, such as Woodcuts and Rotherley in Cranborne Chase, and Marnhull in Dorset, pit-storage continued through the Belgicised phase, though not into the Roman period.[4]

Associated with the pits at Little Woodbury were amorphous scoops or hollows, named 'working-places' by Bersu, who suggested that such tasks as threshing or winnowing might have been carried out in them. While not so immediately recognisable as the storage pits as distinctive features of

[1] I am much indebted to Mr Collin Bowen for his help in considering the problem of 'Celtic Fields' in relation to the thesis presented here. Cf. now his remarks in *Arch. News-Letter* VI, no. 2 (1955), 35.

[2] Grain-storage in pits is still practised in Mediterranean areas, and Diodorus Siculus (V, 21), deriving his information from Poseidonius, refers to underground corn-storage in Britain in the mid-first century B.C. 'They make their harvest of cereals by cutting off the ears and hoarding them in underground structures, from which they take the oldest ears day by day and get food by working them.'

[3] F. H. Worsfold, *PPS* IX (1943), 28–47

[4] C. F. C. Hawkes and M. R. Hull, *Camulodunum* (1947), 48; C. F. C. Hawkes, *Arch. J.* CIV (1947), 27–81; A. Williams, *Proc. Dorset Nat. Hist. & Arch. Soc.* LXXII (1950), 20–75

the Woodbury economy, they can be identified in settlements apart from the type-site.

Bersu further demonstrated that the masses of burnt flints, sooted soil, and clay-oven fragments found thrown into disused pits as rubbish, could best be regarded as the debris of kilns or ovens in which the corn was parched or roasted. Helbaek has taken the matter a stage further in associating the practice with the growing of spelt as a component of the cereal crop, and in giving reasons for regarding finds of carbonised grain as 'accidental products of drying or parching of grain by fire, a process associated with the growing of spelt, which needs such treatment to ensure the easy separation of grains from husks.' Spelt, he goes on to say, 'was the one conspicuous novelty in English Iron-Age plant breeding.' [1] One find of carbonised grain, from Itford Hill in Sussex, shows that the practice (like that of storage pits) did on occasion go back to the Late Bronze Age of southern England.

Evidence of the post-holes for small square granaries for seed-corn, raised above the ground to guard against damp and vermin, and the lines of post-holes interpreted as those of drying-racks, have naturally only been traced in sites where extensive excavation has taken place, but they are recognisable from Sussex to Somerset on half a dozen different farmstead sites, and may be reckoned an integral part of the typical lay-out.[2]

We have then at least five features which recur throughout the farmstead sites in question (apart from ubiquitous stock-breeding), and to this we may add the evidence of grain-rubbers or querns. While not unequivocal evidence of grain growing, since they may be used by non-agricultural communities to grind imported corn, their broad significance must be that of an adjunct to an economy based on cereal crops. The saddle-quern type goes back to the Bronze Age, and the

[1] H. Helbaek, *PPS* XVIII (1952) 194–233

[2] For granaries, S. Piggott, *Arch. J.* XCVI (1939), 220–1 : add R. E. M. Wheeler, *Reports of the Research Committee of the Society of Antiquaries of London*, XII, *Maiden Castle, Dorset* (1943), pl. VII, and A. Williams, op. cit. 29

earlier forms of rotary quern are characteristic of the culture under discussion.

We have defined a well-characterised agricultural economy, with mixed farming predominantly based on corn-growing, strikingly represented in Sussex and Wessex, and with a life-span of some four and a half centuries before the Roman Conquest of A.D. 43. Our next step is to consider how far we can define the geographical limits of this economy in Britain. For this purpose the elements most likely to survive and be recognised are field-systems and storage pits, evidence of corn-parching and the use of the pre-Roman types of rotary quern. If the assumption of the wide-spread occurrence of stable agricultural communities in the pre-Roman Iron Age is to be justified, we should find these elements, singly and in combination, scattered all over Britain, and supplanting the simpler agricultural traditions of the Bronze Age.

The evidence of the 'Celtic Fields' is, as we have seen, tricky in the extreme. Field-systems are difficult to date, and typology may be misleading. Nevertheless, an attempt must be made to map the known distribution of field-systems certainly or probably of pre-Roman date, and those within the period of the Occupation. Such a generalised map, prepared with the help of Mr Collin Bowen, is presented in Map 1.[1] And with whatever allowances may be made for loss of evidence due to recent cultivation and afforestation, the uneven character of archaeological field-work in different areas, and other factors, there can hardly be any doubt that in broad terms the picture presented must approximate to a real distribution-pattern. The areas of concentration are confined to Wessex and Sussex, and in these areas alone is there good evidence for any extensive cultivation of such fields before the first century A.D. Beyond, evidence for the actual existence of such field-systems is at best extremely scanty, and, where evidence

[1] The map utilises many sources, including the unpublished work of Mr R. J. C. Atkinson and the Historical Monuments Commission for Dorset, and that of Mr L. V. Grinsell for the Wiltshire Victoria County History. Notable studies are those by G. A. Holleyman, *Antiquity* IX (1935), 443–54, in Sussex and by P. P. Rhodes, *Oxoniensia* (1950), 1–28, in Berkshire.

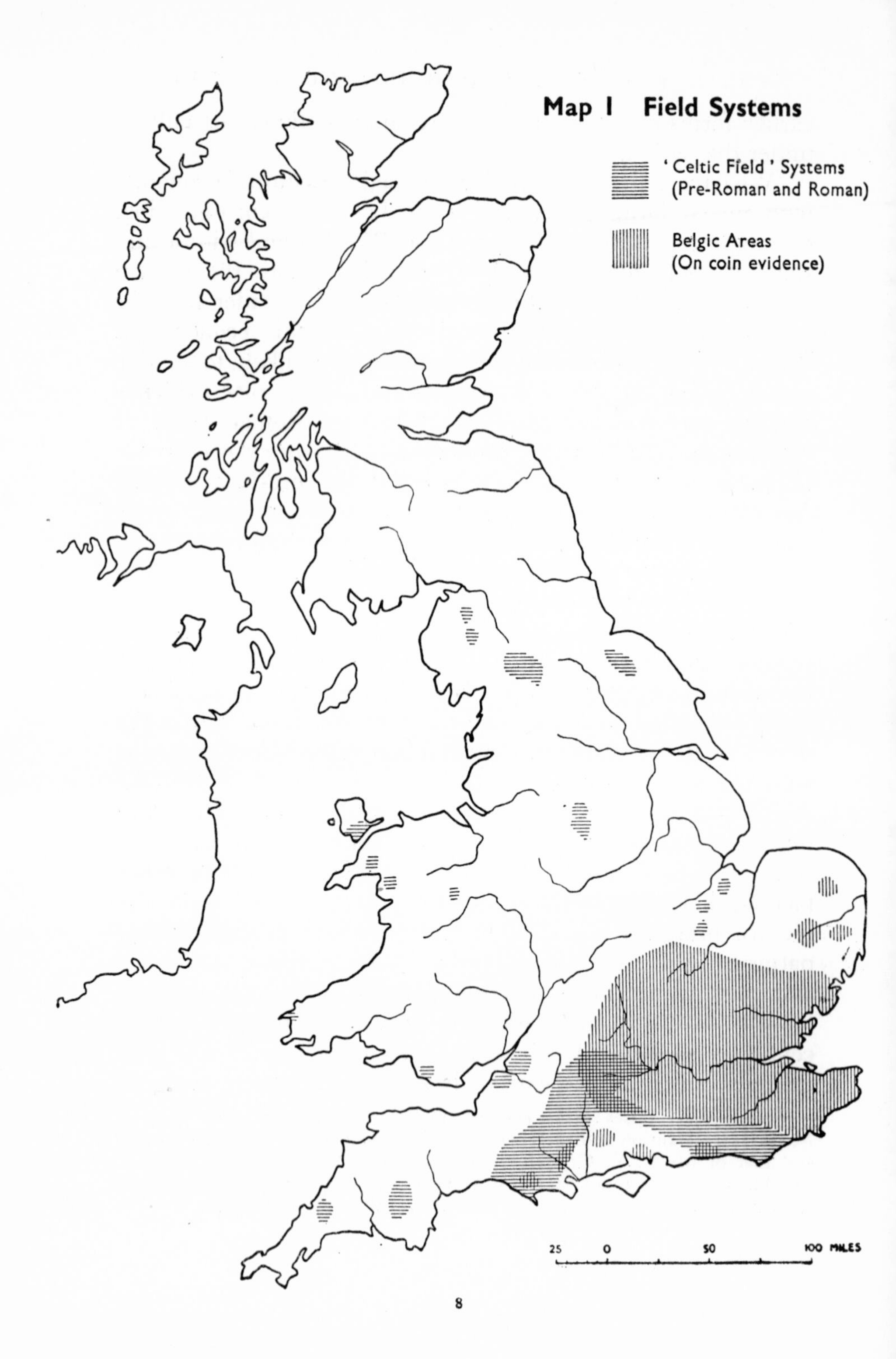
Map I Field Systems
' Celtic Field ' Systems
(Pre-Roman and Roman)
Belgic Areas
(On coin evidence)
25
0
50
100 MILES

of date can be obtained, it is normally within the Roman period.[1]

The fallacies inherent in the use of purely archaeological data are, however, strikingly brought out at one point. For one area on our map devoid of 'Celtic Fields,' that of the Belgic area of the Thames estuary and Kent, there is unequivocal literary evidence that, despite the lack of visible field-systems, corn-growing was carried on to a significant degree; Caesar's testimony to the crops in Kent which enabled his armies to live off the land shows that a map based solely on the evidence of field archaeology may be misleading.[2] As we shall see below, however, the very restricted pattern of the field-systems can be amplified to some extent by considering the distribution of other elements in the Woodbury type of economy. For the present we must leave the question of the fields, returning to consider the question in its specifically North British aspect at a later stage.

There are enough records of Iron-Age storage pits (about 100 sites) to make it likely that their distribution can be regarded as significant. As will be seen in the map (Map 2), the distribution of this feature of the Woodbury economy shows a major concentration coinciding with the field-systems, but extends the area of this type of agriculture into the Middle Thames valley, beyond the north escarpment of the Berkshire Downs where the fields end, along the line of the Ickneild Way in the Chilterns, and along that of the Jurassic Ridge into Northamptonshire. Beyond the boundary of this Ridge, in fact, the Woodbury economy, in so far as it may be denoted by fields or pits, cannot be traced.[3]

[1] One must reckon of course with areas for grazing farm stock within the 'Celtic Field' systems: Rhodes has commented on this in the Berkshire Downs region (op. cit. 8, 21–2).

[2] *B.G.* IV, 32; V, 8. Cf. p. 21 below. The Belgic area is indicated on the map on the evidence of coins.

[3] My map was prepared before Mr C. A. R. Radford published his in *PPS* XX (1954), 11; the very slight divergences in detail between our two versions after correlation are due to my increasing the number of sites in Wessex and omitting a few elsewhere where I did not feel convinced that the pits were in fact of grain-storage type.

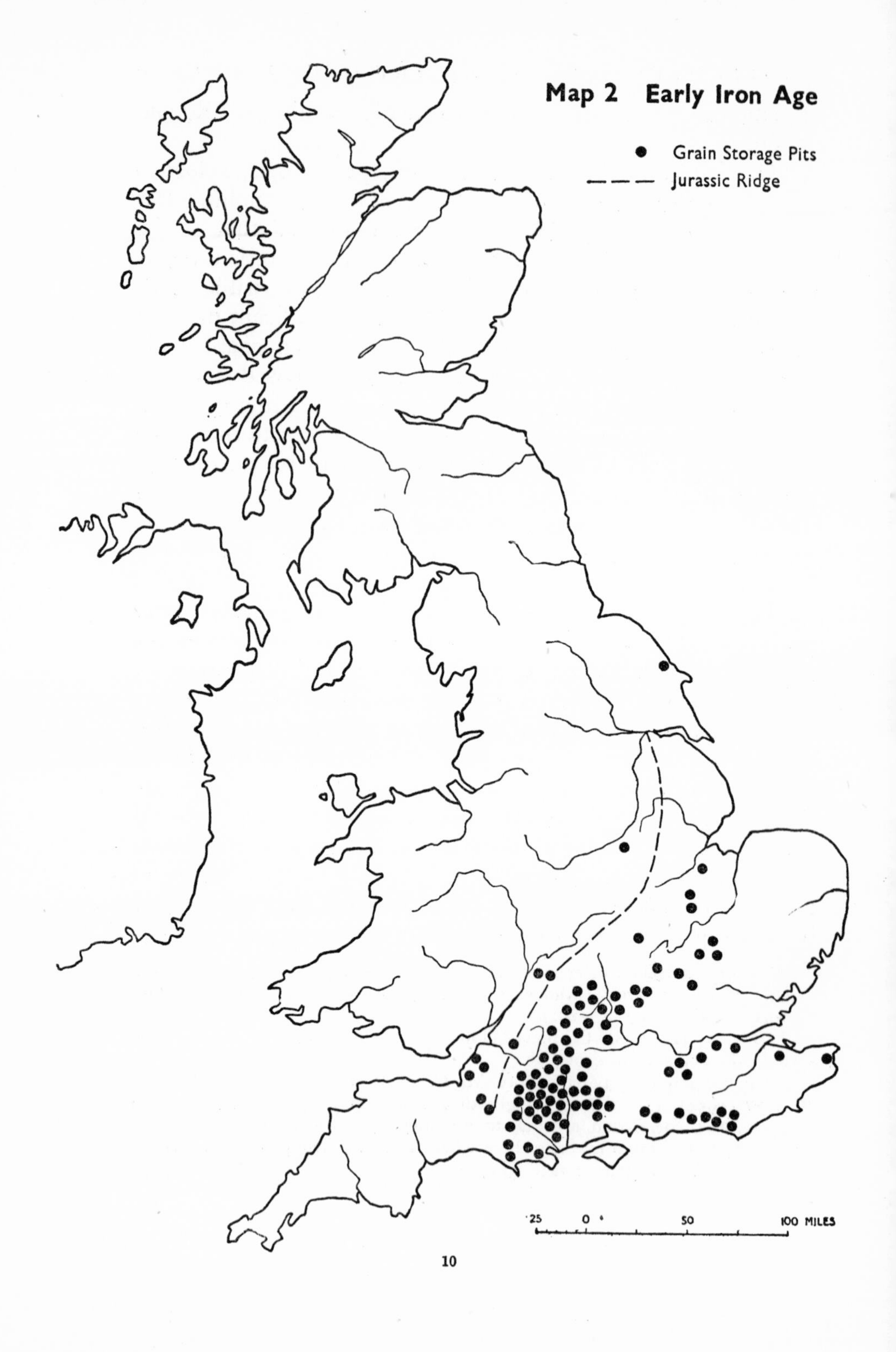
Map 2 Early Iron Age
Grain Storage Pits
Jurassic Ridge
25
0
50
100 MILES

There remains the evidence of querns. Here the preponderance of unassociated and the frequency of vaguely located finds [1] renders interpretation difficult. But the main facts are plain: there is a concentration of pre-Roman rotary quern types within much the same area as that indicated by field-systems and storage pits, and there is a noticeable thinning out of finds in such regions as Derbyshire, Lancashire and Yorkshire. The Scottish evidence is discussed in greater detail below, but it may be said here that it is difficult on the available evidence to regard the appearance of the rotary quern north of the Tyne as an event antedating by many years the Roman crossing of the Humber.[2]

The evidence of carbonised grain must be touched on here, though the relatively few finds render it of less value than the other elements discussed above. It is noteworthy that all pre-Roman carbonised grain finds come from within the area defined above, and that those from Yorkshire and Scotland are Roman (or even later) in date.[3] As is well known, there appears to be no continuity between the Iron-Age use of corn-drying ovens and that of Roman date, the latter being

[1] Cf. J. T. Philips, *Trans. Leicester. Arch. Soc.* XXVI (1950), 75–82; county locations only for nearly half the sites listed as producing querns of the Hunsbury and allied types.

[2] Similar conclusions from the distribution-evidence of storage pits and querns had been reached independently by Sir Mortimer Wheeler, in reviewing the evidence from his excavations at Stanwick, before the writer put forward his thesis in a lecture at Dumfries in July 1953. Sir Mortimer most generously made available to me the typescript of his final Stanwick report, and it is very gratifying to find that, unknown to each other, we had drawn almost identical inferences as to the economic diversity of different areas of Iron-Age Britain. See R. E. M. Wheeler, *Reports of the Research Committee of the Society of Antiquaries of London*, XVII, *The Stanwick Fortifications* (1954), 28–30.

[3] K. Jessen and H. Helbaek, *Cereals in Great Britain and Ireland in Prehistoric and Early Historic Times* (Copenhagen, 1944); H. Helbaek, *PPS* XVIII (1952), 194–233. The pot found with burnt grain on the Culbin Sands (Callander, *PSAS* XLV (1911), 158–81) and said to be of Bronze-Age date is in fact equally likely to be native ware within or after the Roman period; the Camp Hill (Glasgow) find, formerly believed Roman, now seems almost certainly medieval (H. Fairhurst and J. G. Scott, *PSAS* LXXXV (1951), 146–57). The recent finds of burnt grain in what is apparently a late Neolithic context in Shetland may be related to the wet-weather drying referred to below.

consistently of third- and more often fourth-century date.[1] We must also reckon with two forms of grain-drying, one traditional, and resulting from a technique originally devised for spelt, and the other a function of a damp climate and poor sunlight in North Britain, where the technique persisted until recent times: the southern boundary of the practice seems to have been, appropriately, on the Northamptonshire Jurassic! [2]

In sum, therefore, our inquiry has resulted in the discovery that the Woodbury type of Iron-Age economy, associated with intensive corn-growing and distinctive methods for the preparation and storage of the threshed grain, and often taken as typical of Britain as a whole at the eve of the Roman Conquest, is in fact a specialised form of agriculture having a restricted distribution: beyond its limits, more primitive forms of agriculture of Bronze-Age origin presumably persisted. On the whole, its north-west boundary is the Jurassic Ridge, and, on the evidence of distribution and associations alike, it seems likely that this specialisation is a product of the Iron-Age A type of culture, having (with other elements in the same complex) its roots in the Deverel-Rimbury and allied intrusive Late-Bronze-Age cultures of Wessex and Sussex.[3] What then was the economic content of other areas of Britain, and can these be assessed in terms of the other subdivisions of our Iron Age?

[1] R. G. Goodchild, *Ant. J.* XXIII (1943), 148–53; N. E. S. Norris and G. P. Burstow, *Sussex Arch. Coll.* LXXXIX (1950), 1–56

[2] W. L. Scott, *Antiquity* XXV (1951), 196–208

[3] Compare the map showing the extent of the Iron-Age A culture in W. J. Varley, *Arch. J.* CV (1948), 41–66. Documentary evidence, as we have seen, shows Kent and the Lower Thames as corn-producing areas in the first century B.C. The status of the Icenian and Trinobantian areas is obscure, though Belgicisation must have meant good corn-crops, as those encountered by Caesar. But note the possible evidence in Dio commented on below (p. 17).

III

North of the heavily wooded Midland plain, where pre-Roman occupation of any kind is likely to have been scanty or transient, or both, we come into the well-known area of Brigantian hegemony, a vast area under one tribal denomination at the time of the Roman Conquest, though the Parisi of East Yorkshire and the inferred tribe of Setantii in the Ribble Valley [1] suggest that smaller tribes may have existed to be submerged in a Brigantian confederation, though another reason for the exceptionally large size of Brigantia is put forward below.

The archaeology of this area shows that there were, as early as the middle fifth century B.C., communities practising the Woodbury type of farming at least on the east Yorkshire coast. But sites such as Scarborough are quite exceptional in the area, and our evidence, mainly from graves, suggests the survival of ultimate Bronze-Age traditions until the arrival, probably in the middle of the third century B.C., of immigrants whose culture is that of the Continental La Tène I and II phases, constituting in Britain one of the earliest components of our Iron Age B. This Arras Culture of East Yorkshire, with its chariot-graves and its fine metal-work, must lie behind the Brigantian culture [2] as we know it in the first century A.D. at such sites as Almondbury or Stanwick, or from stray finds of metal-work.

In assessing the character of the Brigantian economy we are unfortunately without the abundant documentation afforded by the numerous excavated sites of the Woodbury type, and much of our inference must be based on negative, rather than on positive, evidence. However, the absence of accidental finds of storage pits within the area, and still more significantly,

[1] Ptolemy's *portus Setantiorum*, *Geogr.* II, 3, 2, the Wyre estuary, implies such a tribe. For discussion see Richmond, *JRS* XLIV (1954), 44.

[2] S. Piggott, *British Prehistory* (1949), 162; *PPS* XVI (1950), 1–28, for Brigantian metal-work

their non-appearance within the inhabited area at Stanwick, despite relatively large-scale excavation, suggests strongly that grain-storage did not form a part of the normal economy; and with this would go the lack of field-systems, notably on the Yorkshire Wolds, where the terrain is so similar to that of the Wessex and Sussex downland. Field-systems of Iron-Age type are indeed known in certain areas of the West Yorkshire limestone,[1] but in no instance can a pre-Roman date be demonstrated; as we have seen, all finds of carbonised grain from Brigantia or farther north are of Roman or later date. Rotary querns are few, and need none of them be pre-Roman, while the use of saddle querns simply shows surviving Bronze-Age traditions, also perceptible in the irregular plots of hoe-cultivation type (as on Dartmoor) recorded by Elgee in the North Yorkshire moors.[2] There seems, then, singularly little archaeological evidence for anything more than a continuance of Bronze-Age agricultural techniques in what we call for convenience the Brigantian area, until the introduction of more advanced techniques after the Roman crossing of the Humber.

There is, however, evidence which suggests that an economy which, unlike that of Woodbury, was not specifically concerned with intensive corn-growing, but was primarily centred on flocks and herds, flourished beyond the line of the Jurassic Ridge. I would suggest that we must recognise in Iron-Age Britain, side by side with the Woodbury type of economy, another based on pastoralism and with a probable element of limited nomadism, which may best be called the *Stanwick Type* of economy. At the type-site Wheeler has demonstrated that the great earthwork enclosures must be related to a necessity of rounding up and protecting cattle during the last phase of the Venutian resistance to Rome,[3] and the great dyke systems of the Yorkshire Wolds recorded

[1] Eliot Curwen, *Antiquity* II (1928), 168–72; A. Raistrick and S. E. Chapman, *Antiquity* III (1929), 165–81

[2] F. Elgee, *Early Man in North-East Yorkshire* (1930), ch. xv

[3] R. E. M. Wheeler, *The Stanwick Fortifications* (1954), esp. 27–30

by Mortimer [1] can best be interpreted as in some sense related to some form of ranching involving cattle and, as we shall see, probably horses as well. Independently of the writer, Lady Fox has put forward a case for regarding certain large earthwork enclosures in south-west England, again beyond the effective bounds of the Woodbury economy, as representing cattle-pounds for a predominantly pastoral group of Iron-Age people.[2]

A characteristic feature of the material culture of the La Tène Celts, and of their representatives in Britain, is the use of the horse-drawn chariot as an engine of war. The chariot-burials of chieftains in Yorkshire emphasise this aspect, and the densest concentration of objects connected with or indicative of chariotry in Iron-Age Britain lies north and west of the Jurassic Ridge, or along its line. The breeding of chariot ponies can have been no haphazard affair, as Caesar's tribute to the virtuosity of the Belgic charioteers and their steeds bears witness; careful selection of strains must have been made, and the ponies, when broken in, trained to perform the exacting evolutions of the battlefield. The forces of Cassivellaunus, even when most had been disbanded, still included four thousand chariots, and so double this number of horses.[3] We are prompted to ask where the Belgic remount stables were, and from what sources were their trained battle ponies obtained. They had adopted chariot warfare after their arrival in England [4] and one can only conclude that this reversion to tactics which had long been outmoded on the Continent was the result of contacts with the Parisian or Brigantian peoples, pastoralists and horse-copers, who retained the skills of the old chariot warfare. One may even go so far as to suspect a strong Brigantian element among the charioteers in the Belgic armies, whether as mercenaries or

[1] J. R. Mortimer, *Forty Years' Researches* (1905), 365 and map opp. p. 1

[2] A. Fox, *Arch. J.* CIX (1952), 1–22

[3] *B.G.* v, 19, 'dimissis amplioribus copiis, milibus circiter quattuor essedariorum relictis, itinera nostra servabat.'

[4] S. Piggott, *British Prehistory* (1949), 192

incorporated by other means. But at all events it is to the largely uncultivated lands of Brigantia that one naturally looks when seeking a likely area for large-scale horse-breeding in Iron-Age Britain.

Some corroboration of the foregoing suggestions is afforded by literary evidence, both classical and native. A well-known comment by Caesar, that 'the people of the interior do not, for the most part, cultivate grain, but live on milk and meat and are clothed in skins,'[1] lost favour with archaeologists after the demonstration of the advanced farming system of Iron-Age Wessex and Sussex; but Lady Fox has pointed out that it may well be a true description of a pastoral people comparable to the Masai of East Africa. Strabo's remarks confirm Caesar's observation (if both do not derive from a common source): he adds that some of the inhabitants of Britain, 'though possessing plenty of milk, have not skill enough to make cheese, and are totally unacquainted with horticulture and other matters of husbandry.'[2] Such mobile semi-pastoral economies were again encountered by Caesar in his campaign against the Germans—they 'are not an agricultural people, and live principally upon milk, cheese and meat,'[3] he wrote, and noted of the Suebi that even the farming population moved yearly and that here again 'not much corn indeed is consumed; the people live principally on milk and meat, and spend much time in hunting.'[4] Strabo, indeed, is even more specific in his references to the economy of this tribe and their neighbours. 'It is a common characteristic of all the peoples in this part of the world,' he wrote, 'that they migrate with ease, because of the meagreness of their livelihood and because they do not till the soil or even store up food, but live in small huts that are merely temporary structures; and they live for the most part off their flocks, as the Nomads do,

[1] *B.G.* V, 14, 'interiores plerique frumenta non serunt, sed lacte et carne vivunt pellibusque sunt vestiti.' [2] *Geogr.* IV, 5, 2

[3] *B.G.* VI, 22, 'agri culturae non student, maiorque pars eorum victus in lacte, caseo, carne consistit.'

[4] ibid. IV, 1, 'neque multum frumento sed maximam partem lacte atque pecore vivunt, multumque sunt in venationibus.'

so that in imitation of the Nomads, they load their household belongings on their wagons and with their beasts turn whithersoever they think best.'[1] Tacitus, too, noted the German fondness for cattle in terms which might well have been written of the Masai—they were poor undersized beasts, but 'the Germans delight in quantity, and these are their only riches, which give most pleasure.'[2]

The antithesis between meat-eating savage and bread-eating citizen is ancient in classical thought, and in the speech put into the mouth of Boudicca by Dio the contrast between the Romans, who cannot exist without their bread and wine and oil, and the Iceni, who have no need of more than the raw products of rude Nature,[3] may well, in this set piece of rhetoric, be nothing but a well-worn trope. But it may, on the other hand, embody a reminiscence of actual Roman commissariat problems brought about by the occupation of an island inhabited only in part by corn-growing agriculturalists; and this is a point to which we will return.

The evidence of archaeology implies that the background of the material culture reflected in the earlier Irish tales of the Ulster Cycle is broadly speaking a version of the Brigantian Iron Age as represented in Northern Ireland from about the first century B.C. Conditions of life as depicted in these stories, then, would approximate to that enjoyed by the immediate ancestors and relatives of Cuchulainn in Britain. And there is no doubt that in the Cattle-Raid of Cooley, and in the other Ulster stories, we are among the warrior aristocracy of a pastoralist economy. When Medb and Ailill vie in displaying their wealth one to another, after the household gear and personal ornaments are brought forward they survey their stock of sheep, horses, pigs and cattle in this order: the whole tale, of course, turns on a cattle-reiving.[4] There

[1] *Geogr.* VII, 1, 3

[2] *Germ.* 5, 'numero gaudent, eaeque solae et gratissimae opes sunt.'

[3] Dio, LXII, 5, 'every grass or root is corn to us; every juice, oil; every water, wine.'

[4] T. P. Cross and C. H. Slover, *Ancient Irish Tales* (New York, 1935), 284

is no need here to go over the evidence in detail, for the general picture is well known. Whatever may have been the status of the lower orders of society, the heroes of the Ulster stories at the beginning of the Christian era are chariot-driving pastoralists, counting their wealth in flocks and herds.

It seems reasonable to assume, therefore, that beyond the limits of the Woodbury type of agriculture there existed, wholly or in part, an alternative Iron-Age economy based on pastoralism, which we have named from the site of Stanwick in Yorkshire. There seems a fair case for identifying such an economy in Brigantia, and Lady Fox would see a counterpart to it in south Wales and south-west England. By and large, it would march with the territory of the Woodbury economy along the Jurassic Ridge, and would be one, perhaps the dominant, aspect of the Iron-Age B culture. Within its area, agriculture is likely to have been limited to hoe-cultivation in the Bronze-Age tradition, preserved among a substrate population. Pasturage on a large scale demands extensive territories, and the great size of Brigantia may be a reflection of its dominant economy, in which a limited degree of nomadism, perhaps seasonal, may have taken place.

It has been argued that pastoral nomadism can only exist on the fringe of a settled agricultural economy with which it can trade, or into whose territory it can raid.[1] Whatever the relationship between the two economies in Britain, trade must have played an important part, and, as we have seen in the instance of the Belgic charioteers, other contacts could also have been established. The warrior aristrocracy of a pastoral economy forms the ideal patron for the armourer and metal-smith, and Fox's map of fine metal-work and chariot-graves in Iron-Age Britain shows a broad arc of finds stretching from east Yorkshire along the Jurassic Ridge into Somerset: the map in fact demonstrates the frontier zone of maximum trade

[1] R. K. Beardsley, *American Antiquity* XVIII (1935), 24–8: *Memoirs of the Society of American Archaeology*, No. 9. I have discussed the matter in the wider setting of Old World prehistory in Chapter I of *The Metropolis in Modern Life* (ed. R. M. Fisher, New York, 1955).

between the two economies suggested above,[1] and we see how a mere handful of fine metal-work finds lies within the main area of the Woodbury economy in Wessex and Sussex.

IV

If, then, we accept as a working hypothesis that Iron-Age Britain contains two main economic zones, that of the Woodbury type of farming south and east of the Jurassic Ridge, and that of the Stanwick type of cattle-ranching north and west of that line, what of the lands beyond Brigantia? The northern edge of this tribal area is notoriously difficult of definition, but is likely to have lain somewhere along the Tyne–Solway line, on the southern edge of the Cheviot massif. The Southern Uplands and the Midland Valley of Scotland approximately comprise the area up to the Antonine Wall; north-east to the Moray Firth accessible lands skirt the uninhabitable Highland mountain block, and on the west the Atlantic sea-ways link the Islands and Highlands to Orkney and Shetland.

The main content of the Scottish Iron Age has been discussed elsewhere by the present writer,[2] and it is sufficient to say here that chronologically it seems highly probable that the greater part of Scotland and much of Northumberland at least remained in a retarded Bronze-Age cultural tradition up to the first century B.C. When elements representative of the southern Iron-Age cultures did arrive north of Brigantia they seem largely to have been carried by refugee populations, numerically small but militarily competent, who established themselves as overlords.

Although among the novel equipment of these invaders rotary querns of southern English types seem to have been

[1] C. Fox, *The Personality of Britain* (4th edn., 1943), fig. 12. Cf. his map analysing the source of objects in the Llyn Cerrig hoard, *A Find of the Early Iron Age from Llyn Cerrig Bach* (Cardiff, 1946), fig. 34 and comment, p. 63.

[2] S. Piggott, in *The Problem of the Picts* (1955), 54–65

introduced, these need denote no more than an improved technique of flour-milling, more effective than the traditional saddle quern: they cannot be used as evidence for any innovations in agricultural methods. No trace of field-systems of Iron-Age or Romano-British type can be found, except in one or two exceptional instances which are on other grounds to be regarded as of Roman date.[1] Two or three iron plough-shares of Belgic type have been found in southern Scotland, but again in Roman contexts.[2] On the whole we can only accept the evidence that, as in the area of the Stanwick economy, corn-growing remained at a Bronze-Age level at the time of the Roman Conquest of North Britain. That the intrusive Iron-Age overlords shared the pastoralist economy of Brigantia can be inferred, though one would expect some attempts at stable agriculture to be encouraged by chieftains who had come from within the ambit of the Belgic or the Woodbury economies. But the absence of storage pits in Scottish Iron-Age sites shows that any direct transference of Woodbury techniques is unlikely.

Although the Scottish Lowlands would permit of the use of field-systems approximating to those of the Woodbury economy, it must be remembered that in such areas of distinctive Iron-Age cultures as these of the brochs and wheel-houses of the Atlantic Iron Age, hoe cultivation or the use of such a tool as a caschrom is far better adapted to local conditions: here the very nature of the terrain prohibits much improvement in agricultural techniques beyond a rather primitive level. But for large tracts of Scotland we may well have to accept at face-value the low standards ascribed to the Maeatae and Caledonii by Dio, who, for all their charioteering, lived in rough shelters, went naked and barefooted, 'having neither walls nor towns nor tilth, but living by pasturage and the chase, and on certain kinds of nuts,' though not eating fish.[3] The Bronze-Age evidence shows that cereal crops,

[1] Cf. Curwen, *Antiquity*, VI (1932), 402. I cannot accept the alleged lynchets at Torwoodlee (V. G. Childe, *Scotland before the Scots* (1946), 83).

[2] F. G. Payne, *Arch. J.* CIV (1947), 82–111

[3] Dio, LXXVI, 12

especially barley, had been grown in Scotland since early in the second millennium B.C.,[1] and one must assume that such cultivation continued until the eve of the Roman conquest, but the yield can never have been high.

V

The concept of Iron-Age Britain outlined above, with the potential grain harvest rapidly decreasing as one moves inland and crosses the line of the Jurassic outcrop, to drop even more markedly when the regions north of the Tyne–Solway line are reached, demands a re-assessment of the relationship between Roman and native, town and countryside, army and civilians. In a well-known series of papers some twenty-five years ago such problems were discussed by Collingwood and others in relation to the estimated population of Roman Britain,[2] but this was at a time when the Iron Age was represented by 'pit-dwellings' and 'British villages.' Can we now see the situation a little more clearly?

The Roman army, and for that matter the civil population who had accepted Mediterranean habits of life, saw corn and bread as the basis of existence. The army rations were in corn, cooking-fat and wine, and while the last would have to be almost wholly an import into Britain, the Claudian chiefs of staff must have proceeded on the reasonable assumption that their forces could in very large measure live off the land. And this was not based on a guess that Britain would closely resemble Gaul in its agricultural economy, for Caesar had apparently provided the hard facts: his army of some 12,000 men had, in the first expedition, supported itself on the local corn for a fortnight, and in the second there had been a successful levy from the Trinobantes of grain for a considerably larger force. Any further intelligence reports would inevitably have described agricultural conditions in the

[1] K. Jessen and H. Helbaek, op. cit., maps on p. 47

[2] R. G. Collingwood, *Antiquity* III (1929), 261–76; H. J. Randall, ibid. IV (1930), 80–90; R. E. M. Wheeler, ibid. IV (1930), 91–5

Lowland Zone, and given accounts of the Belgic or of the Woodbury type of economy.

While the line of the Fosse Way is not that of the Jurassic Ridge, it sufficiently approximates to what we have considered as the north-west frontier of the Woodbury economy to be worth considering in economic terms. The Roman consolidation in the Lowland Zone, apart from the campaigns into the Welsh Marches, spans about a generation from the Conquest. The Brigantes were made a client kingdom, however insecurely; the Silures were kept at bay. Within the area bounded by the Fosse, native agriculture was already geared to a respectable level of corn-production which could be encouraged and intensified. Within the same area, too, the beginnings of Roman farming based on the villa could utilise soils unattractive to the native economy. What was to take shape as the civil portion of the Roman Province was in fact its granary.

Archaeology confirms the historical inference. Pitt Rivers' excavations of farmsteads in Cranborne Chase produced the evidence, newly interpreted by Hawkes, that 'in the earlier part of the Roman period, when the inhabitants were still maintaining the pre-Roman practice of drying their consumption-grain and storing it in pits, a large part of their harvest was taken away from them by official Roman requisition.[1] By the second century, pit-storage is given up altogether. Bersu estimated, from the Woodbury evidence, that the annual consumption-harvest there was about 55 bushels; on similar evidence the Rotherley farmstead, round about A.D. 10–45, was producing some 64 bushels, Woodcuts the same amount as Woodbury. Bersu's figures indicate a farm of about 20 acres of arable, allowing for a proportion of fields lying fallow each year, and 50 acres is likely to be the maximum that could be tilled by a single household.[2] To quote specific

[1] C. F. C. Hawkes, *Arch. J.* CIV (1947), 79

[2] Cf. L. D. Stamp, *The Land of Britain* (1948), 339 ff. for modern farm sizes. The Rockbourne Down enclosure included 96 acres and had three corn-drying kilns in the third–fourth centuries A.D. (Hawkes, op. cit. 35*n.*) but some of this area was presumably pasture.

cases, surviving areas of field-systems of Iron-Age or Romano-British type in the Berkshire Downs total nearly 8,000 acres; in Dorset some 30,000 acres. Even if only two-thirds of this area was under cultivation at any one time during the Roman period, the grain output must have been well in excess of the needs of the native population.

We may consider for a moment the question of corn consumption in its relation to cultivated areas in the south of England. Bersu's figures were based on an estimated Iron-Age yield of one-third the modern corn crop on chalk, which came out at about 11 bushels per acre. This, as a matter of fact, agrees well with the Roman estimated yield (as given, for instance, by Columella), of 9 bushels per acre. Ten bushels per acre would then be a good round figure to work on. From this Bersu deducted one-third again for seed-corn, and so arrived at the annual consumption-harvest of around 7 bushels per acre. In calculating the arable for the Woodbury farm he further allowed for a two-year fallow, and in suggesting its population used the modern figure of 4½ bushels per head per year.

These estimates also agree well with what has been deduced from medieval documentary sources; Beveridge's figures for A.D. 1200–1450 indicate a yield per acre of 9·36 bushels of wheat, 10·56 bushels of oats, and 14·32 bushels of barley, and for any given manorial area he would halve the annual yield to allow for lands left waste. He too estimates the seed-corn at one-third of the yield.[1]

These figures may be used to give us rough approximations of output and consumption in Roman times: the Dorset yield, using the factors indicated above, might be expected to produce something like 46,500 bushels of grain a year, which would be enough to feed 10,000 persons. Looking at it from the other point of view, a Roman legion would need about 500 bushels of corn a week, or the crop off a little over 70 acres. The provisioning of Caesar's first expedition in Kent (10,000–12,000 men for a fortnight or so) would have involved

[1] W. H. Beveridge, *Econ. Hist.* no. 2 (1927), 155–67

the corn crop of about 300 acres of land—the annual produce of perhaps twenty to twenty-five farms.

The advance into Brigantia, and the subsequent Agricolan campaigns, must have depended upon elaborate arrangements for providing the armies with corn grown in the Lowland Zone. The North British campaigns must be considered in terms of this logistic problem, for there is little likelihood that at any point beyond the Humber the Roman forces could obtain locally grown grain in any quantity; indeed, it is far more probable that no surplus whatever was produced by the little hoe-cultivated plots of ultimate Bronze-Age husbandry.

In this connection, we must look for evidence of deliberate Roman policy in corn production in Britain. Both Collingwood and Hawkes have thought that in Cranborne Chase we may recognise an Imperial estate, at first concerned with grain-growing by encouraging (and depleting the granaries of) the native farmers. In the Fenland it looks as though a completely new area was turned over to corn by means of a drainage scheme which can only be attributed to Roman organisation, and in this context the evidence of the local Roman canal system, represented by the Car Dyke and likely to have been in the main devoted to barge shipment of corn northwards, appears (in Stukeley's words) 'one of those consummate strokes of policy and public utility, for which the Romans were so famous.' Professor Grahame Clark's excavations have shown that the Car Dyke was cut as early as *c.* A.D. 50–60, continued in use until the end of the second century, and had ceased to function by the late third century A.D.[1] It is impossible to dissociate this evidence, as Clark points out, from the problems of provisioning Lincoln and York, and the whole circumstances of the northern campaigns.

So far as the Scottish campaign was concerned, it seems likely that most of the corn would have been shipped up the east coast to points such as Inveresk and, more significantly, to *Horrea*, the granary by very definition, at Carpow on the

[1] J. G. D. Clark, *Ant. J.* XXIX (1949), 145–63

Tay. Such trade is likely to have been carried on, in part at least, in native craft and by native seamen used to traffic on this route, and the appearance of Belgic types of iron-work in southern Scotland, and of armlets likely to be of Romano-Belgic inspiration in the North-East, may not be unrelated.[1]

In the relationship between Roman and Native in North Britain, then, one must bear in mind that the Romans were on the whole campaigning in territories in which, while there may have been abundant flocks and herds, there was only the most rudimentary agriculture, of a type hardly likely to produce any surplus over home consumption. This circumstance would inevitably control all military movement in Scotland, and the establishment of shore bases on Forth and Tay emerge immediately as crucial events in the campaign. By these alone could effective supplies be brought in from the corn-growing areas to the south-east, since the opportunities for establishing effective farms in Scotland were small, and dependent on long-term considerations.

It is likely, however, that some stimulus to improved farming may have been given in the Lowlands, where such pieces of evidence as the plough-shares already mentioned exist, and sites like Tamshiel Rig in Roxburghshire, a stone-built version of a Woodbury type farmstead with thirty acres of adjoining fields, while highly exceptional, nevertheless show that on occasion local corn-growing may have been encouraged and improved, perhaps by Iron-Age refugees from southern England before the Roman campaigns. On the whole, though, the Roman occupation of Britain north of the Humber (and in large areas to the west, such as Wales) must have meant the imposition of a military force not only alien in origins and traditions, but in the basic economics of its existence. The Celtic cow-boys and shepherds, footloose and unpredictable, moving with their animals over rough pasture and moorland, could never adopt the Roman way of life in the manner of the settled farmers of the South.

[1] Cf. S. Piggot, *PSAS* LXXXVII (1952–3), 1–50

VI

It is perhaps permissible, as a postscript to the main thesis presented here, to turn for a moment to the Roman attitude to just this pastoral economy in the North. Since Collingwood first put forward the suggestion,[1] the idea that in later Roman times there was a change-over from intensive corn production to sheep-breeding in southern England has been received favourably, and Hawkes' new work on the Cranborne Chase material has brought forward corroborative evidence.[2] There seems in fact to be some evidence that the woollen trade was encouraged under Imperial auspices in the North as well.

The archaeological evidence for native Iron-Age weaving styles, notably the characteristic bone combs used to pack the threads on the loom, shows that such cloth manufacture, going back to southern England to at least the fourth century B.C., was also carried out in later times in Brigantia and farther north.[3] Between the Humber and the Forth a number of finds have been made, frequently in contexts dating them to the period of the Roman Occupation: more specifically, they can be shown to range from the first to the fourth century A.D. And farther north, such weaving was typical of the builders of brochs and wheel-houses in the Atlantic Iron Age of Scotland, with an approximately similar range of date, and the terracotta model of a votive bale of wool from a broch in Skye points directly to a Roman interest in the crofters' industry of the time.[4] Even if formally outside the Empire, trade might still be carried on, and the production of wool encouraged, in the Islands and elsewhere north of Hadrian's Wall, and the west Yorkshire evidence for fourth-century

[1] R. G. Collingwood and J. N. L. Myres, *Roman Britain and the English Settlements* (1936), 223–4

[2] C. F. C. Hawkes, *Arch. J.* CIV (1947), 32–3, 71

[3] Cf. map in A. S. Henshall, *PPS* XVI (1950), 130–62, fig. 5

[4] V. G. Childe, *Scotland before the Scots* (1946), 84

communities of Romano-British shepherds and weavers in the limestone hills around Settle suggests again that the high quality of British woollen cloaks attested by Diocletian's 'Edict of Prices' a little earlier may owe something to a cloth industry in the North. The Cheviots were certainly supporting sheep by St Cuthbert's day, and British cloaks still held their own in the European markets of the eighth century.[1] Northerners knew the need of these things, and the three cloaked and hooded figures on the relief from the Housesteads *vicus* may in more ways than one be symbolical of the British herdsmen and shepherds whose chariot-driving ancestors, *pollentes nobilitate*, had counted their wealth in cattle and sheep before Cuchulainn had become a legend.

[1] Cf. Carus Wilson, in *Cambridge Econ. Hist.* II (1952), 360–3

Chapter II

ROMAN AND NATIVE, A.D. 80–122

IN A.D. 43 the Emperor Claudius launched his invasion of Britain, a project which, ever since the raids of Julius Caesar a century earlier, had never been completely shelved.[1] By A.D. 47 the first phase of the invasion was successfully over. Southern England had either been subdued or had passively submitted, and a forward line had been established across the country from the Humber to the Bristol Channel. That line was presently marked by a Roman military road, the Fosse Way, running along the Jurassic Ridge, an immemorial communication route between north-east and south-west.[2] At either end of the line the legions had already established bases, the Ninth at Lincoln, another at Gloucester,[3] while a central army group, consisting of the Fourteenth and another legion, lay in the Midlands, ready to thrust north-westwards towards the Chester area and the sea. This movement, designed to drive a wedge between the still unsubdued North and West and to secure a sea-base for further operations, provoked a hostile reaction among tribal units of the adjacent North, and from this point the known story [4] of Roman and Native in North Britain begins to unfold.

The first chapter of the story here considered deals with the period from A.D. 47, when hostile contact is first recorded, till A.D. 122, when Rome, having penetrated far into the North, had withdrawn with a sharp realisation of the difficulties and of the excessive drain on man-power involved. The area

[1] C. E. Stevens, in *Aspects of Archaeology* (1951), 332–44

[2] W. F. Grimes, ibid. 144–71

[3] C. Green, *JRS* XXXII (1942), 39–47 : for the legion, see Richmond, *JRS* XLIV (1954) 48

[4] For vague references to other episodes, see A. Momigliano, *JRS* XL (1950), 41–2 : cf. C. E. Stevens, *Class. J.*, N.S. I (1951), 7–9

covered is roughly the whole sweep of land north of a line joining York, Derby and Chester, a region so different from the South in geography and in archaeological background that its treatment as a purely military zone follows from its special nature.[1] From A.D. 47 to A.D. 71 only the southern portion of the region came within the orbit of Roman authority, and even so only as a protectorate. An advance in stages followed, culminating in Agricola's victory over the massed native forces of the North at Mons Graupius in A.D. 85, whereupon the country up to the Grampians was occupied and organised under military control. After his recall the northern fringe of that occupation was curtailed; and finally, soon after the turn of the century, there came a hasty withdrawal of the Roman forces to south of the Cheviot, a position which in A.D. 122 was consolidated by the great work of Hadrian's Wall. The whole picture is of vicissitude and experiment, but it is not in the Roman world abnormal. Both the barrier protectorate,[2] to shut off hostile areas beyond, and the type of occupation once a conquest was haltingly made, are matched on other frontiers of the Empire. Indeed, the solutions found for problems in Britain are best understood against the wider background of Roman frontier policy and administration as a whole. The fact that no part of Northern Britain ever became a fully developed civil province, is to be set against similar policies upon other frontiers, where over and against unconquered territory, the same military administration was established. Such occupied zones served as buffers to absorb the shock of war and prevent its surges from flooding into the areas of the full Roman peace. In them the degree of Romanisation, even in the most favoured areas, was slight; the immediate requirement was security, and any degree of Romanisation achieved was a by-product of the occupation rather than its purpose.

[1] The classic exposition of these differences is Sir Cyril Fox, *The Personality of Britain* (4th edn.), 1943.

[2] E. Kornemann, *Gestalten und Reiche* (1943), map 2 has a memorable phrase for this policy, *unsichtbaren Grenzen*; cf. his *Weltgeschichte des Mittelmeerraumes* II (1949), 160.

The Roman attitude towards native peoples in such areas had nothing in common with modern humanitarian sentiment. Security attained, there followed the exploitation of natural resources in metals or any other useful commodities, such as timber, hides, animals and slaves. The areas also became reservoirs for the supply of irregular troops, as this arm was developed in the Roman military organisation.[1] But the profession of any aim to ameliorate the native lot, so common in the dealings of modern nations with native peoples, was absent. Benefit enough if Rome brought and enforced the habit of peace, as Cerialis very bluntly reminded [2] the rebels in the revolt of Civilis. As for the loss of freedom, the scornful comment of the Elder Pliny is instructive.[3] Having pictured the life of the Chauci on their Dutch mud-flats, dwelling in huts twice daily surrounded by the tides, without herds, eating fish and drinking only laboriously collected rain-water, without proper clothing or means of fire, he concludes, 'And these are the people who talk of being reduced to slavery, if they are vanquished by Rome!' A different attitude is found only in those Roman writers in whom the Stoic influence was strong, as, for example, the utterance of Seneca on human values and the glorification by Tacitus of the virtues of German life, uncorrupted by civilisation. The conception of the Roman dominion as a *Völkerbeglückungspolitik* [4] was beginning to take shape, though its clear expression lay far ahead. In the first century such ideas are to be dismissed as reveries of literary men.[5] Velleius Paterculus, a hardened soldier who knew frontier warfare, spoke with the authentic Roman voice when he described natives as 'Creatures who have nothing but men's voice and limbs.' [6] If in the West the native reaction anywhere found articulate expression, we do not know of it. Only in the East, among men imbued with religious ideas quite

[1] G. L. Cheesman, *The Auxilia of the Roman Imperial Army* (1914), 18

[2] Tac. *Hist.* IV, 74 [3] *Nat. Hist.* XVI, 4

[4] Kornemann, *Weltgeschichte des Mittelmeerraumes*, II, (1949), 133

[5] Alföldi, *CRFS* (1949), 4: the first clear Christian statement of Imperial duty comes from Melito of Sardes, towards the end of the second century.

[6] II, 129, 3

alien to Roman thought, was voice found for hatred of Roman rule. Hoping for the day when the wrath of God would make an end, the writer of the Apocalypse saw in all Rome's power only a traffic of gold and silver and all precious things, in slaves and the souls of men.[1]

Yet though insensitive and callous by modern humanitarian standards, Rome was not deliberately brutal in her treatment of native peoples. In his political testament Augustus, the founder of the Empire, declared that he had preferred, wherever possible, to preserve rather than to destroy—'*externas gentes, quibus tuto ignosci potuit, conservare quam excidere malui*'[2]; and his declaration on this matter, as on many other points acquired the force of precept for his successors. Whenever native tribal organisation reached a sufficiently advanced stage and co-operation was forthcoming, the disturbance of the native pattern of life was often surprisingly slight.[3] But where resistance was implacable, extermination brought no qualm. Fire and sword brought peace in Britain as elsewhere if there seemed no other way. Such was the fate of the Welsh Ordovices[4]; such had been the fate of the Cantabri in Spain and the Salassi in the Alps before them.[5] Ruthlessness towards civilians might incur official check,[6] as in Southern Britain after the revolt of Boudicca, when Suetonius Paulinus was deliberately removed. The set policy was essentially that of Peace, and to that end, as Mommsen[7] put it, 'the implications of the situation' formed the only guide. It is then, in the light of the implications of the situation that Roman policy in the North between A.D. 47 and A.D. 71 must be interpreted. Having reached the Fosse Line, the Roman advance northwards halted there for twenty-four years, because the situation rendered further advance unnecessary, and because the conquest of Wales on the flank was a prior necessity.

[1] *Rev.* XVIII, 13 [2] *Mon. Anc.*, 3

[3] As in Scotland at Traprain Law, in Wales at Tre'r Ceiri, or in Gaul at Bibracte [4] Tac. *Agr.* 18 [5] *CAH* X, 344, 348

[6] Tac. *Ann.* XIV, 38; cf. Tiberius, Sueton., *Vit. Tib. Caes*, 32 *boni pastoris esse tondere pecus, non deglubere* [7] *Staatsrecht* III (1887), 826

The name Brigantes,[1] as ancient writers call the folk of northern England, seems to have been used for a number of tribal groupings in loose confederacy, under the leadership and often imperfect control of rulers whose authority centred in the West Riding of Yorkshire. The population comprised a wide variety of cultural elements,[2] especially in the North-West, forming in general terms a rather stagnating Bronze-Age society [3] ruled by foreign princes of Iron-Age culture who had intruded from the South or South-West. Conditions varied greatly, from primitive savagery at the barest subsistence level among scattered cow-herds inhabiting the bleak uplands,[4] to a certain barbaric splendour among their chiefs. Although recently a barbaric coinage had begun to circulate, the penetration of goods from the relatively more civilised South was surprisingly small. Only the Parisi of the Humber area had begun to import fine articles such as Arretine pottery before the conquest.[5]

The lost books of Tacitus may have described first Roman contacts with the Brigantes, but his later references make the story plain. As soon as the invading troops reached the Fosse line, the Brigantes became a client kingdom. This meant that Rome did not proceed with her conquest northwards, while the Brigantian rulers for their part adopted a pro-Roman policy, preserving the peace and offering no asylum to refugees. But there was a dangerous corollary. Rome held herself free to interfere, not only if summoned in support of the native rulers, should their policy prove unpopular, but also in case of any disorder or misgovernment which threatened the frontier peace. The establishment of client kingdoms, which was standard Roman policy at this time, in the main achieved its intended purpose, a maximum of peace with a minimum

[1] Kitson Clark, *YAJ* XXXIV (1938), 80–7; Richmond, *JRS* XLIV (1954), 43–52

[2] E. Birley, *CW*² XXXII (1932), 137

[3] W. J. Varley, *Arch. J.* CV (1948), 62; cf. V. G. Childe, *Prehistoric Communities of the British Isles* (1940), 245–7

[4] Raistrick, *YAJ* XXXIV (1938), 148–9. The fox and otter were eaten.

[5] Corder and Davies Pryce, *Ant. J.* XVIII (1938), 262–77; for spelling of Parisi see Ptolemy, *Geogr.*, II 3, 10

expenditure of Roman military strength. The effective working of the arrangement was assisted sometimes by subsidies paid to the native rulers, sometimes by the presence of a resident Roman official,[1] sometimes by a quartering of Roman detachments.[2] The arrangement fostered the admission of Roman traders with reasonable security, and sometimes the exploitation of natural resources in the area by Roman *entrepreneurs*.[3] The arrangement lasted, however, only as long as the implications of the situation might decide. At the very time when Rome was initiating such a kingdom in North Britain, she was terminating one in Thrace and setting up another in the Crimea.

The course of events among the Brigantes did not run smoothly. The Queen, Cartimandua, and her consort, Venutius, had cast in their lot with Rome and their policy had been so unpopular that Tacitus, commenting upon events in A.D. 51, states that Roman military support had long been required, a reference to the Brigantian 'discords' which interrupted the campaign of Ostorius Scapula in north Wales in A.D. 47. The Roman general had turned back, killed the troublesome few who had taken up arms, and the disorder settled down. Presently Ostorius struck a formidable blow in Wales, by bringing the native leader, Caratacus, to a decisive battle; and when Caratacus, defeated, fled north to Brigantia seeking asylum, he was at once handed over to Rome,[4] a dastardly act which stank in native story [5] for a thousand years. But, from the Roman point of view, the policy in the North was bearing fruit.

The antecedents of Didius Gallus, the next Governor, may here be thought significant.[6] He came to Britain from the command of Moesia, a province then adjacent to potentially troublesome kingdoms in various forms of loose association with Rome. It had fallen to him during his command to deal

[1] As in Thrace, *CAH* x, 645
[2] Tac. *Ann.* XII, 45
[3] Cf. Roman *negotiatores* in Bohemia, Tac. *Ann.* II, 62; Roman mining beyond the Rhine, Tac. *Ann.* XI, 20; or a *procurator* at Rottenburg, *ILS* 8855
[4] Tac. *Ann.* XII, 36–7
[5] Casson, *CW*² XLIV (1944), 68–80
[6] *CAH* x, 752–3

with dynastic struggles both in the Bosporan kingdom, and in Thrace, supporting a native prince in one and annexing the other. He thus came to Britain well versed in the handling of difficult frontier situations and with an excellent record of success, at a time when a Welsh settlement was of the first importance, while in the North it was necessary to foster a friendly understanding. If Didius, then, arrived with instructions to pacify Wales and to maintain an understanding with the North, his capacities were soon to be tested. The Welsh remained no less obdurate than before, while among the Brigantes the immediate development was a dynastic feud between Cartimandua and her consort Venutius,[1] the foremost British warrior, according to Tacitus, after Caratacus. When a personal quarrel broke out between them, Didius did not treat the matter too seriously, sending at first auxiliary troops to restore peace, but needing in the end the services of a regular legion,[2] presumably the Ninth from Lincoln. In his earlier account of the incident, in the Histories,[3] Tacitus, writing of events of the year A.D. 69, says that trouble was then brewing in Britain, instigated by Venutius, who now hated both the Roman name and Cartimandua. He then tells briefly the background story of the Brigantian civil war, when Cartimandua, quarrelling with Venutius and marrying his armour-bearer, was turned out of her kingdom, though rescued by Rome. But the later account, in the Annals, makes it clear that a first quarrel, afterwards patched up, took place about A.D. 57. The prestige and power of Cartimandua endured and were strong enough to keep the North quiet during the Boudiccan revolt of A.D. 61.

Meanwhile, however, archaeology has taught us something of northern politics at this time, through the recent excavation of the *oppidum* at Stanwick [4] and of some hill-forts on the

[1] For the state of affairs among the Brigantes and their coinage, see Richmond, *JRS* XLIV (1954), 43–52

[2] Tac. *Ann.* XII, 40

[3] Tac. *Hist.* III, 45

[4] Sir Mortimer Wheeler, *Reports of the Research Committee of the Society of Antiquaries of London*, XVII, *The Stanwick Fortifications* (1954)

Scottish Border.[1] Stanwick lies near Catterick in North Yorkshire, where converge the natural routes from the north-west, across the Pennines by way of Stainmore, and from the north, through Northumberland and Durham. This is an area of ancient and obvious strategic importance, where opposing forces from North and South have often met. Here Sir Mortimer Wheeler has elucidated a complex of earth-works which, starting from a nucleus of 17 acres, grew by successive stages to cover first 137 acres and then 600 acres. By native standards, or indeed by any standards of that age, the final form is huge : it implies, in the words of the excavator, 'a powerful, and in Northern Britain unique, concentration of tribesmen and their economy (note the careful inclusion of the best local water-supply within the vast fortifications) at what can only have been one of these rare but recurrent moments of crisis which produced simultaneously a strong Celtic leader and a momentary unification.'[2] The intermediate *oppidum* of 137 acres yielded pottery indicating strong Roman contacts in the third quarter of the first century, while the final enlarge-ment had been hurriedly undertaken to meet an emergency. Sir Mortimer accordingly relates the first enlargement to the period A.D. 57–71, when Venutius had settled his first quarrel but lived in his own centre, and the last huge fortification to the crisis arising when the Roman armies advanced in A.D. 71 and tribesmen rallied to Venutius from far and wide in order to stay that advance. As for farther north, Professor and Mrs Piggott have recently distinguished in the Scottish Borders a burst of fortification, of a type matched not in Scotland but farther south[3]; and the finds suggest that the authors were groups of refugee warriors, probably not even accompanied by their women-folk. A picture thus begins to emerge of a northern focus of resistance stretching from Yorkshire to southern Scotland, to which were attracted all who abhorred Roman dominion. Of this political grouping Stanwick, commanding the northward road, was the ultimate

[1] C. M. Piggot, *PSAS* LXXXII (1947–8), 222–3 [2] *Ant. J.* XXXII (1952), 9
[3] *PSAS* loc. cit. ; also LXXXIII (1948–9), 63

focus and, as Sir Mortimer Wheeler has pointed out,[1] there is evidence of the variety of elements finally assembled there. This northern stronghold would in fact represent the *oppidum* of Venutius. Cartimandua was nevertheless the suzerain, and her kingdom, with Roman support, served for more than a decade after the troubles of A.D. 57 as a buffer state effectively shutting off the restless North. On the existence or extent of Roman penetration in support of her, however, there is no clear answer. The early fort at Templeborough, near Rotherham, seems to date to about A.D. 60, but other evidence is lacking.

The *modus vivendi* between Venutius and Cartimandua thus represents the settlement of Didius Gallus. It lasted, however uneasily, until the death of Nero in A.D. 68 plunged the Roman world into a civil war, in which three Emperors rose and fell within a year before the purple finally rested on the shoulders of Vespasian. In Britain, the sympathies of the legions were divided. The Governor, Bolanus, did not send support to Vitellius, though appointed [2] by him ; and upon this Tacitus comments [3] that Bolanus was the sort of general who wished his men to love him, and that he was too gentle for a turbulent province like Britain. The first comment is obviously a gibe at the governor's indecision ; the second indicates that he had some trouble to deal with, and has been connected with the fact that a generation later, the poet Statius,[4] writing a poem to Bolanus' son who was then starting a military career, recalls the achievements of his father in Britain and speaks of the military works he established, the breastplate he took from a British king, and mentions the Caledonian fields, implying that his exploits lay in the North. When all allowance for the poetic cliché is made, it is reasonable to conclude [5] that Bolanus did conduct a campaign in the North to which reference could be made within the family circle. In general terms, Tacitus states that the North took heart on hearing of the civil war within the Empire and the divided sympathies of

[1] *Ant. J.* XXXII (1952), 13
[2] Tac. *Hist.* II, 97
[3] Tac. *Agr.* 16 and 8
[4] *Silvae,* V, 2, 144–9
[5] Cf. E. Birley, *Roman Britain and the Roman Army* (1953), 13–15

the Roman troops in Britain, and that Bolanus interfered to check the trouble which was brewing. He did not, however, press such success as he gained, thereby incurring the disparagement of Tacitus, who measured every Roman general in Britain by the example of his idolised father-in-law, Agricola. Tacitus also indicates that Cartimandua took drastic action, casting off Venutius as her consort and marrying his armour-bearer. This, as already noted, (p. 34), precipitated a violent quarrel, in which tribal loyalties passed to Venutius. Cartimandua was rescued with difficulty, and Tacitus summed up the result : *regnum Venutio, bellum nobis relictum.*[1]

The war came as soon as Vespasian controlled the situation. Cerialis, well experienced in the North as Officer Commanding the Ninth Legion a decade earlier, returned as Governor of Britain in A.D. 71 and undertook a final settlement of the Brigantes. The campaign, Tacitus states, was bloody, but most of the tribe was either conquered or overrun.[2] The main objective was presumably the anti-Roman block extending from North Yorkshire to the Scottish Borders. In that case we would suppose a double movement of Roman troops, one arm advancing up the west side of the Pennines, the other up the east and over Stainmore, where the marching-camps of an advance preceding the Roman road can still be seen.[3] The stronghold of Stanwick would be dealt with in the eastern advance, which caught its defences not fully prepared. The point of convergence of the two movements would be the Eden valley. Here Carlisle[4] has long been known to have yielded pottery of distinctively early character as compared with Corbridge, where the pottery of the later Agricolan movement is relatively abundant. With part of the forces established at this advanced base, the remainder would probe and penetrate the invaded area.

[1] Tac. *Hist.* III, 45 [2] Tac. *Agr.* 17

[3] Reycross and Crackenthorpe : Richmond and McIntyre, *CW*[2] XXXIV (1934), 57 ; Plumpton Head : St Joseph, *JRS* XLI (1951), 54

[4] Bushe-Fox, *Archaeologia* LXIV (1912–13), 295–314. *JRS* XI (1921), 201–2 refers to tiles of the Ninth Legion from Scalesceugh, five miles south of Carlisle, but their date and purpose are alike obscure.

But if Carlisle was an advance base, what further operations were conducted from it? Evidence within the last few years indicates that these operations extended into Upper Annandale at least, wherever else similar evidence may yet be found. At Milton (General Roy's Tassiesholm), near Beattock, Roman troops constructed a substantial fort,[1] abandoned some years before the well-known Agricolan advance. It is difficult to see to what occasion this fort can be referred, if not to Cerialis' campaign. Thus a possible and exact interpretation of the words of Tacitus may be offered. The area conquered would be north England, south of Stainmore, with a forward base at Carlisle; the area overrun would be the territory to the north-west, including Annandale.

It is well to realise what such operations meant to the native population. Brief historical summary will state that a tribe was conquered, or a district was overrun, but it is important to visualise what this implied. A vivid picture is offered by the Dacian campaigns, conducted by Trajan in the mountainous country of the Carpathians, where Rome was subduing a similar freedom-loving and warlike population. On the Triumphal Column erected in Rome official artists depicted both the campaign and the work of pacification.[2] Many of the scenes are grim. A Roman force returns, each man holding in his hand [3] the severed head of a foe; in the same battle scene [4] a soldier deals with an enemy, while holding the head of another in his teeth; here a native village [5] is set on fire, while the inhabitants scatter in flight; there a crowd of captive natives [6] stands dejectedly within a walled concentration area; yet again appears the breaking-up [7] of native families, men going one way, women and children another. Roman soldiers are building works [8] near which, in warning, the heads of

[1] *Trans. Dum. & Gall. Ant. & Nat. Hist. Soc.* XXVIII (1949–50), 205–6; cf. *JRS* XLI (1951), 123, fig. 15

[2] C. Cichorius, *Die Reliefs der Traianssäule* (Berlin, 1896–1900), vol. I. The Arabic numbers quoted below are of scenes.

[3] op. cit. Taf. xviii, 58

[4] op. cit. Taf. xix, 59–60

[5] op. cit. Taf. xx, 63–4

[6] op. cit. Taf. xxxviii, 113–14

[7] op. cit. Taf. lvi, 200–1

[8] op. cit. Taf. xl, 140

natives are placed on poles. No conquest is without its Quislings: a telling scene[1] depicts the surrender of a group of natives with their chief at a fort-gate, while peeping slyly over the wall and whispering together, two Dacian Quislings watch the scene. Fighting in set battle without much quarter on either side, grim work in patrols, the burning of villages and the flight to hill and forest, heroism and treachery, destruction of the familiar pattern of life: such in Dacia was the conquest, and such without doubt among the Brigantes. And the fighting over, what then? Submission of a proportion of the notables and their slow assimilation into the new scheme of things; flight for the intransigent to the North, in the hope that they might at least remain free; for ordinary folk the gradual and cautious return to ruined homesteads and a picking up of the threads of daily life. Then would follow changes of which archaeology cannot speak; the drafting of likely lads to service in distant auxiliary units of the Roman army; the requisitions of grain, often made harshly and unfairly, an evil with which Agricola tried to cope and one evidenced by the false measure found at Carvoran[2] and the false weight at Loudoun Hill[3]; taxes on persons, land and property as assessed by the *census*; forced labour[4] on Roman works, such as the great roads. All these represent a minimum. There might be expropriation where it suited the Roman authorities to clear an area of native population or where the land was assigned for use to a fort garrison. Cumulatively the burden was heavy, and long resented. It was still possible nearly a century later to stage a serious revolt, when the destruction of the fort at Ilkley and the rebuilding of other Yorkshire forts, tell a story of unsettled conditions persisting from early in the occupation.

[1] op. cit. Taf. lv, 199; it is not certain, in the opinion of Cichorius, that the so-called Quislings are connected with the surrender [Ed.].

[2] Haverfield, *AA*³ xiii (1916), 85. The question whether this measure, officially certified, is really inaccurate is by no means certain [Ed.].

[3] R. P. Wright, *JRS* xxxvii (1947), 180, no. 8. Mr Wright draws my attention to the fact that the weight is only 6 % short, and that this is not an uncommon error, perhaps unintentional [Ed.].

[4] Tac. *Agr.* 31

As to the Roman reaction, Tacitus has composed two expressions of native feelings, one by the Caledonian leader, Calgacus,[1] the other by the Batavian rebel, Civilis.[2] He puts into their mouths complaints of the insatiable greed of Rome, the loss of freedom, the grinding injustice of taxation and requisitions, and the cruelty of military drafts. As for the vaunted Roman peace, 'They make a desert and call that Peace.'[3] So Tacitus, seeking to express what he imagined a native felt. But to the hard-bitten Cerialis, victor in the Batavian revolt, it appeared otherwise. 'You never knew peace and security,' he reminds the rebels, 'till Rome came. And peace you cannot have without soldiers, and soldiers you cannot have without pay, nor pay without taxation.'[4] To Cerialis the logic of Roman conquest was complete.

There were many collaborators, probably the majority in all ranks of society. At the upper levels of society it was the Roman method to allow tribal organisation to function where sufficient collaboration could be found and where sufficient social integration already existed. Occasionally, it has been argued, Rome went further and created or fashioned anew tribal organisation to serve her purpose.[5] In the North we have little evidence in the early years either of such effective collaboration or of such Roman creativeness. Generally speaking, the Romans found it necessary to dismantle native centres of any importance. The defences of Almondbury[6] were demolished and the same fate overtook Carrock Fell.[7] At Aldborough there came into existence the town of Isurium Brigantum, evidently the centre of tribal administration, as organised by Rome, but there is no evidence that this stage was reached in the settlement immediately following conquest. At one place only in the North is there evidence of a town early adopting Roman ways, and that is at Brough-on-Humber

[1] Tac. *Agr.* 30–2
[2] Tac. *Hist.* IV, 14
[3] Tac. *Agr.* 30
[4] Tac. *Hist.* IV, 74
[5] W. T. Arnold in *Studies of Roman Imperialism* (1906), 155
[6] *JRS* XXX (1940), 166
[7] Collingwood, *CW*[2] XXXVIII (1938), 41

where, in the territory of the Parisi, a new town was created about the turn of the century, and where Marcus Ulpius Januarius, aedile of the *vicus* of Petuaria, honoured Antoninus Pius by providing a theatre-stage for the community.[1] There was perhaps a hope originally of more rapid Romanisation than proved possible. A Greek school-master, Demetrius, was attached to the staff of Northern Command Headquarters at York with the possible function of organising the education of young British nobles along civilised lines.[2] At the lower levels of society, the natives flocked round the Roman forts, to form settlements which finally attained official status as *vici*.[3] There natives felt themselves in touch with the big world and the novelties of civilisation and could profit thereby: there was, for example, a concentration of native metal-working round the fort at Kirkby Thore.[4] But the bulk of the population must have been scattered in villages and remote, isolated homesteads where the Roman influence came near to vanishing point, and contact with the conqueror was limited to the exactions of the Roman officials on their rounds. Tacitus states that the Britons were good tax-payers, provided they were not treated unjustly.[5] It may be that the Brigantes shared this doubtful praise; we do not know. Taxes were in theory the Imperial Government's share of the increment in value accruing from the Roman peace, and the quite intensive cultivation [6] of the fertile Yorkshire dales may be indeed evidence of that increment. But throughout much of the North the flocks and herds which might be taxed in money or kind elude our estimate, and it is in any case likely that the expense of the occupation must have greatly exceeded the return. The occupation was undertaken out of military necessity and remained by force of circumstance military, since the adjacent lands to the north never, except for two comparatively short periods, passed fully under Roman

[1] *Ant. J.* XVIII (1938), 198; *YAJ* XXXIV (1938–9), 99
[2] *CIL* VII, p. 62; *ILS* 8861: cf. Richmond, *JRS* XXXIV (1944), 44
[3] Cf. *ILS* 7003, 7004, 7049, etc.
[4] RCHM, *Westmorland* (1936), p. xxxix
[5] Tac. *Agr.* 13
[6] *JRS* XL (1950), pl. VI, 98

control. The real return lay in the security which the occupation afforded to the civil South.

There must in fact have been wide areas where tribal organisation was either insufficiently developed or insufficiently co-operative, and in such circumstances administration as well as police control must have devolved upon fort commanders. We know that, in Derbyshire, Brough-on-Noe was such an administrative centre [1]: and that there is the possibility that the local inhabitants [2] were designated as 'men of Anavio,' and not by any tribal name. Fiscal functions of forts are indicated by evidence from Newstead, in Scotland,[3] at a much later date, and from Ribchester.[4] It seems probable that this method of administration was a general one. But not every fort commander, good soldier though he might be, could be expected to deal competently with all the problems which might arise; even his superiors at district Headquarters or at Command might err. Imperial Procurators in the course of their multifarious duties could smooth out much; but they were no less prone to human weakness and perhaps more venal than officials of higher standing; and one wonders whether the special appointment of *iuridici* [5] to Britain about this time had anything to do with difficulties emerging in the administration by the military of a population accustomed to quite different forms of tribal law. Mr C. E. Stevens has called attention [6] to a curious passage in the Code which may anticipate early Welsh laws of heredity.

Lastly, there is the possibility that some areas, in particular those with mineral wealth, were administered directly by Imperial Procurators as domain land in the hand of the Emperor himself. From the outset of the invasion Rome had been interested in British minerals [7] and their exploitation

[1] *Derbyshire Arch. J.* report forthcoming

[2] *ILS* 1338: cf., however, Richmond and Crawford, *Archaeologia* XCIII (1949), 42, s.v. *Navio*

[3] J. Curle, *A Roman Frontier Post and its People* (1911), 309–10

[4] Richmond, *JRS* XXXV (1945), 28

[5] E. Birley, *Roman Britain and the Roman Army* (1953), 51

[6] *JRS* XXXVII (1947), 132–4

[7] Tac. *Agr.* 12

followed everywhere rapidly upon the advance of the armies. Within six years of the landing the lead mines of the Mendips were in active production,[1] and the fact that pigs from the West Yorkshire lead mines, less productive than those of Derbyshire and less rich in silver, are dated as early as A.D. 80 makes it certain that the whole area began to be exploited[2] very soon after the conquest by Cerialis. The Derbyshire mines are unusual in Britain in that they appear to have been managed by lessees of the Imperial Government,[3] not by the military as was usual. As for the actual mining, we know from Florus[4] and from the Theodosian Code[5] that labour was often supplied by *corvée*, if it did not consist of slaves and criminals under military guard. Fetters found in alleged Roman mines in Yorkshire might be taken to support the latter possibility.[6] At the Matlock mines in Derbyshire there was quite an industrial settlement,[7] whether free or slave we do not know. But we learn something of the organisation of such a community from the regulations at the mining centre of Vipasca in Spain.[8] These regulations, belonging in their present form to the time of Hadrian, are surprisingly complete and cover not only the working and administration of the mine but the retail trades supplying the mining community and the establishment of baths and barbers' shops. Given the general uniformity of Imperial organisation, it may reasonably be assumed that at the mining village of Roman Matlock affairs were ordered in not dissimilar fashion.

The roads and forts of northern England are commonly attributed to Agricola, but the construction of a first strategic network must have been begun by Cerialis immediately after

[1] *CIL* VII, 1202 [2] *CIL* VII, 1207 [3] *CIL* VII, 1214–16

[4] *Epitome* II, 25 (IV, 12), of the Dalmatians: '*efferum genus fodere terras coegit aurumque venis repurgare.*' See O. Davies, *Roman Mines in Europe* (1935), 14, for further examples.

[5] *Cod. Theod.* XI, 7, 7 [6] O. Davies, op. cit., 14–16, 164

[7] W. Gowland, *Archaeologia* LVII (1901), 381–4: VCH *Derbyshire* I (1905), 227–32: for the place-name *Lutudarum*, see Richmond and Crawford, *Archaeologia* XCIII (1949), 38 s.v.

[8] Bruns, *Fontes Iuris Romani* (1909), 289–95; J. J. van Nostrand, in *Economic Survey of Ancient Rome* III, 167–74

his conquest and may indeed have been substantially completed by him, since his successor, Frontinus, was able to turn his whole attention to Wales. Certainty as to the part which each Governor played is impossible because of the difficulty of dating sufficiently closely the foundation of the sites upon the roads concerned. The main lines which they follow are conditioned by the geography of the area. Two trunk roads run northwards on either side of the Pennines and are linked by a succession of cross-roads using the natural gaps. The west road runs from Chester by Manchester, Ribchester and Overborough, up the Lune valley to Low Borrow Bridge, over Crosby Ravensworth Fell to Brougham and so to Carlisle. The east road, starting either from Lincoln, by way of Doncaster and Tadcaster, or from York, passes thence by Aldborough and Catterick to Scotch Corner; there the road forks, one branch, which may probably be the original main course, crossing the Pennines by way of Stainmore to join the west road at Brougham, the other going north by Binchester and Ebchester to Corbridge. The cross links, from south to north, are these: from Manchester through Derbyshire by way of Melandra Castle and Brough-on-Noe to Templeborough and the east road near Doncaster; from Manchester by way of Castleshaw and Slack to the Calder valley and the east road at Castleford; from Ribchester by Elslack and Ilkley to the east road at Tadcaster; from the Overborough area by Brough-by-Bainbridge into Wensleydale; the Stainmore road, already mentioned, from Catterick to Brougham; and the Stanegate from Corbridge to Carlisle. From the west road the coast was reached by two roads, one from Brougham by Ambleside to Ravenglass, the other from Carlisle to Maryport; and farther south Lancaster and Watercrook were established. On the east side, in addition to the main road, another route used ran across the Humber ferry to Brough and on to York with a branch to the North Riding by way of Malton and Cawthorn.

The work of Agricola in the North, to which we may now turn, presents many difficulties, arising now from vagueness

Map 3 Agricola in North Britain

of topographical reference, now from the desire of Tacitus to paint a general picture of his ideal commander, rather than to describe precisely what he did. Doubt is encountered immediately the Tacitean account begins. We are told that after correcting administrative abuses, Agricola gathered together his army and marched into an area hitherto untouched, an area of estuaries and forests. Here he pursued operations, sometimes relentlessly (head-hunting springs to mind), sometimes with clemency, so that the natives submitted without serious fighting.[1] It is commonly supposed that the area referred to is north-west England. This would imply that the campaigns of Cerialis, which we have seen reason to believe extended into Annandale, left this area on his flank untouched, and that it remained untouched in the years of consolidation which followed.[2] Moreover, it is not, except in its southern part, conspicuously a land of estuaries; it is a land of mountains. Nor was it, to judge from the network of roads and forts which controlled it, a submissive area. Rather one inclines to place the campaign in south-west Scotland, which is a land of estuaries pre-eminently and which was an area hitherto untouched. On this suggested reconstruction of events Agricola, having concentrated his forces on Carlisle, would have marched north-west and won the easy conquest which a sparse, unorganised population made natural.

Before he embarked on his next campaign, Agricola spent the winter in an interesting experiment. Knowing that a scattered, uncivilised population is apt to be troublesome, says Tacitus,[3] Agricola decided to give them a taste of the pleasures of civilisation and so win them from their warlike, savage ways. By bringing pressure to bear in private and by public help he set them to build temples, market-places, houses, all in decent Roman style. The co-operators were rewarded with praise; the tardy and obstinate were encouraged in ways they

[1] Tac. *Agr.* 21

[2] The legionary fortress at Chester was not founded before A.D. 78, see *Chester Arch. J.* XXXVIII (1951), 18; until this happened, the western coast-line can hardly have been absorbed [Ed.].

[3] Tac. *Agr.* 21

would understand. The result was that the sons of chiefs took to education in which their natural ability made them apter than the Gauls for all their plodding diligence. Before long the very people who had refused to speak Latin began to have ambitions as skilful users of it. They took to Roman dress and were proud of it. *Facilis descensus*; soon they were spending their time in philosophical discussion, baths, and dinner parties. In their ignorance they called all this culture, comments Tacitus acidly, when it was in fact part of their enslavement.

Such was the experiment. How far it affected the North is unknown. But no doubt something was attempted among those elements of the Brigantian population who were receptive, and within limits it may have succeeded. The development of such a place as Isurium may well have begun so, and even *villae* may have been established thus early in proximity to the fountains of Roman culture. From the Roman point of view Agricola's policy was sound; and it is a fact that, apart from occasional disorders connected with more widespread unrest and a certain insecurity in outlying districts, the Brigantes in the main accepted the Roman peace.

Next spring Agricola set out on the serious invasion of Scotland. If our reading of the previous campaign is correct, his western flank was secure. The main expectation of resistance must have been from the central Borders where, as we have seen reason to believe, die-hard refugee elements had settled. We can trace the advance of one column, apparently the main one, from Corbridge northwards, by the route later known as Dere Street, over the Cheviots to the large fort at Newstead near Melrose, while a secondary column moved from Carlisle up Annandale and upper Clydesdale, the two columns converging on the Forth, possibly at Inveresk. From there the advance continued, apparently by Camelon to the Tay,[1] where a sea-base may have been established thus early at Carpow.

[1] There seems now to be agreement, whatever the exact reading in *Agr.* 22, that the Tay is meant. It does not follow that the Agricolan army as a whole penetrated so far in this campaign (cf. Richmond, *JRS* xxxiv (1944), 39).

While the general pattern of the advance is fairly certain, much detail remains to be confirmed by archaeology. Two things strike us about this movement, its scope and the absence of serious resistance.[1] The scope, remarkable in comparison with Roman field operations in Britain except in the early days of the conquest, is explicable if Agricola was using large mobile forces and relying on supplies conveyed by sea to the Forth and Tay estuaries. The absence of resistance may be explained in various ways: either by lack of native forces, which seems most improbable in view both of the network of forts and roads which the occupying troops immediately created and of the evidence that resistance was being organised in the Borders immediately before the invasion; or by divided counsels among the tribes, as so often in the Celtic world. The second explanation appears the more probably true.

The next year was spent in consolidation. Forts were erected between Forth and Clyde and the whole sweep of land southwards [2] was brought under control. It is to this time that we must date the first period of the Flavian forts now known in southern Scotland—Cappuck, Newstead, Oakwood, Milton, Dalswinton, Glenlochar, Castledykes and Loudoun Hill. The picture awaits completion by further excavation, but already the pattern of occupation is plain, and it was one from which the Romans, in all their subsequent experiments of occupation, did not depart. It consists of two main north and south lines, intersected by two east-west lines, each marked by roads. Between these roads we begin to know some cross-links and may expect the discovery of more.[3] The two east-west roads imply two sea-bases on the west coast, in the neighbourhood of Irvine and Stranraer, neither of which is yet identified. We do not know what relation the pattern

[1] E. Birley, *Roman Britain and the Roman Army* (1953) has emphasised the absence of resistance, but is disposed to attribute it to successful field operations of Cerialis, a view for which there is at present no archaeological warrant. The scope seems far too wide. [2] Tac. *Agr.* 23

[3] The Nithsdale–Crawford road by Durisdeer is certainly Antonine, but its Agricolan date remains without proof. See *Trans. Dum. & Gall. Ant. & Nat. Hist. Soc.*, XXXII (1953–4), 10.

Map 4 The Tribes of North Britain as listed by Ptolemy

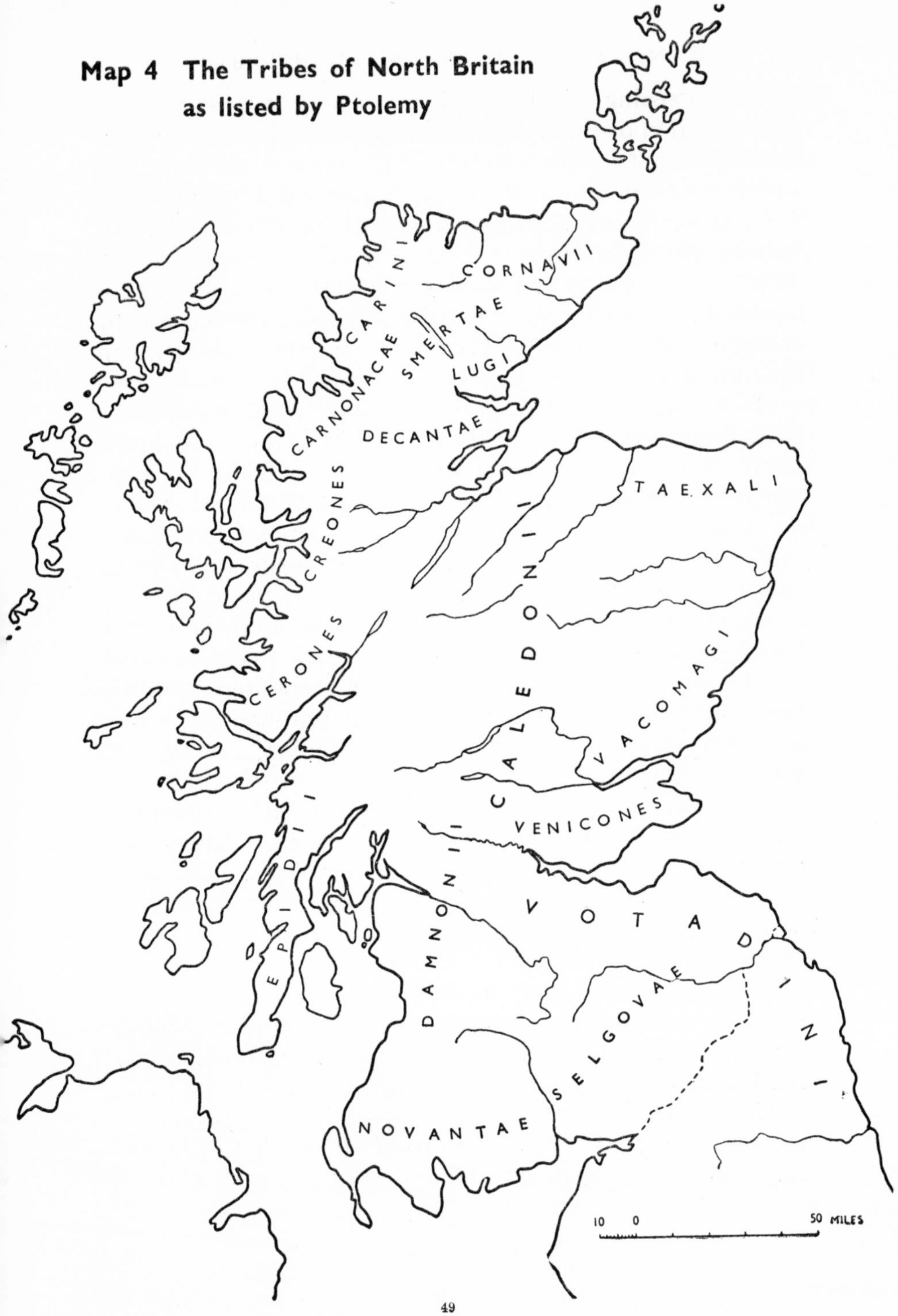

CORNAVII
CARINI
SMERTAE
CARNONACAE
LUGI
DECANTAE
CREONES
TAEXALI
CALEDONII
CERONES
VACOMAGI
VENICONES
EPIDII
DAMNONII
VOTADINI
SELGOVAE
NOVANTAE
10 0 50 MILES

bears to existing tribal groupings. There is a rough compartmentation of the known tribes, the Votadini, the Selgovae and the Novantae, occupying the three southern compartments, and the Damnonii most of the western part north of the dividing line ; but the natural configuration of the area seems to have been a determining factor of considerable effect. The consolidation was attended by the construction of a line of temporary works between Forth and Clyde, barring out the northern tribes. This, as Tacitus prophetically states,[1] might have become a frontier, and later became the Antonine Wall.

In the farther North meantime the common peril had at last enforced unity[2] under the leadership of their own chiefs, aided, one suspects, by refugee princes whose personal experience carried conviction. The North had in fact become the 'last refuge' of the vanquished,[3] whither all the most elusive of the Britons had fled. Agricola assures us that the fighting force they mustered amounted to 30,000 men, an incredible figure. Yet the course of the last campaign is proof that Agricola had now to deal not only with a skill of leadership far above what had previously been encountered but with numbers acting in cohesion and with purpose. We must assume that the whole North had been mobilised ; not only the tribes south of Strathmore but the Broch chieftains of Sutherland and Caithness and perhaps beyond—witness Agricola's concern about the Orkneys before the campaign closed. The patent decisiveness of the last battle shows that here indeed the native leaders staked all. Some twenty years were to pass before the North could again rally to a fresh bid for freedom.

These last campaigns were conducted by Agricola with caution. Aware of the determination and the strength of the North, he made it his first business to seize the points where the Highland passes open into Perthshire, lest hostile forces suddenly emerging thence should take him in the rear. A great legionary base was established to watch the Dunkeld gorge on the Tay at Inchtuthil and a screen of blocking forts

[1] Tac. *Agr.* 23 [2] Tac. *Agr.* 29 [3] ibid. 25, 34

was erected at Fendoch in the mouth of the Sma' Glen, at Dealginross near Comrie, where the Earn leads far back into the mountains, and at Bochastle, near Callander, controlling the Pass of Leny.[1] This cannot be the whole tale of such works, but it is enough to illustrate the tactical principle and the efficiency of the Roman military machine.[2] The excavation of Fendoch reveals the work in all its completeness. Agricola was too good a soldier to make the mistake of seeking to penetrate the Highland Glens. Had he tried, his biography might not have been written, for no hostile army has ever done it with success. Instead he moved forward from Inchtuthil, north-eastwards along the Grampian border to Stonehaven where the mountains almost meet the sea. And here, at the gateway to Aberdeenshire, that fateful battle of Mons Graupius may have been fought. Much ink has been spilt on the question of the site of this battle. It seems impossible that we shall ever know for certain, but the argument [3] for Raedykes, near Stonehaven, is more convincing than most. The site has the necessary strategic significance, for it controls the entry to the whole North-East ; the topography, when compared in detail with what Tacitus says, fits remarkably ; and Tacitus must have had a clear mental picture, having heard the story, no doubt frequently, from his father-in-law's own lips. But two points are troublesome. Raedykes is a short distance from Inchtuthil, only some 60 miles ; yet the Roman army reached the site of the battle only at the very end of the summer.[4] Secondly, if the whole North was in arms, it might be expected that the final battle would have taken place nearer the Broch area, which must have supplied a substantial part of the native force. For these two reasons one would tend to look for Mons Graupius somewhere in the approaches to Inverness. Recent air reconnaissance has partly confirmed,

[1] For a comparable policy in Transylvania, see Richmond, *JRS* XXXI (1941), 204–5 ; for Fendoch, Richmond and McIntyre, *PSAS* LXXIII (1938–9), 110–54

[2] cf. The remark by Josephus, *B.* v., iii, 5 that the Roman camps were erected 'more quickly than thought.'

[3] O. G. S. Crawford, *The Topography of Roman Scotland* (1949), 130–2

[4] Tac. *Agr*. 38

partly revealed a whole series of marching camps beyond Strathmore. It is difficult not to believe that these mark the route, though not necessarily the works, of the Agricolan army.[1] Again, the Latin account indicates that after the battle Agricola did not advance farther, but returned by leisurely stages to base, very literally putting the fear of death into the tribes as he went. From the Boresti, whom W. J. Watson thought to link with modern Forres, he took hostages.[2] If, therefore, Agricola turned back after the battle, and if Forres were his northward limit, Mons Graupius cannot have been fought at Stonehaven. The final episode, a naval descent on the Orkneys and their formal surrender [3] seems a solid fact in support of the thesis that the centre of resistance lay in the extreme North.

At this point the Governorship of Agricola ended. He left Britain secure and safe, as he thought,[4] for his successor. The High Command must have shared his view, for almost immediately a whole legion, the Second *Adiutrix*, was withdrawn for service on the Danube. If it was accompanied by the complement of auxiliary regiments, this would mean a depletion of strength by some 10,000 men. Thenceforward events are obscure. When Tacitus came to write the Histories he remarked bitterly that the Emperor Domitian, among other failures in duty, had let Britain go immediately after the conquest was completed,[5] words which were long taken to imply that, immediately after Agricola's governorship, the Romans withdrew from Scotland. Sir George Macdonald was the first to show [6] conclusively that this interpretation could not be correct; that, on the contrary, Agricola's Scottish conquests continued to be held in force till a date around or soon after A.D. 100. Since then controversy has ranged around two questions, the precise meaning of the words of Tacitus and the date of the withdrawal.[7]

[1] J. K. St. Joseph, *JRS* XLI (1951), 64–5
[2] Tac. *Agr.* 38
[3] Tac. *Agr.* 10
[4] Tac. *Agr.* 40
[5] Tac. *Hist.* I, 2
[6] *JRS* IX (1919), 111–38
[7] Macdonald, *JRS* XXV (1935), 187 ff; XXVII (1937), 93 ff; Davies Pryce and Birley, XXVIII (1938), 141 ff; Macdonald, XXIX (1939), 5 ff

The first question can now be reviewed with more knowledge than was available when Sir George Macdonald wrote. The words of Tacitus are explicit. He says that immediately after the conquest of Britain had been completed (a task which, according to Tacitus, Agricola thought he had accomplished by his defeat of the native armies at Mons Graupius), something happened which could be interpreted as a throwing away of this achievement. There must, then, have been some factual basis for the gibe at Domitian, clearly referable to events immediately following Agricola's campaigns. And it begins to appear that such a basis may exist. Excavation on most Flavian sites in Scotland has revealed two main periods or phases, the second of which everywhere begins with sweeping changes, sometimes indeed with complete reconstruction. At the beginning of this second phase, the defences of Newstead were replaced by others on a much more massive scale; at Dalswinton the fort was enlarged and strengthened; at Milton there was a complete reconstruction of the defences; at Loudoun Hill a new fort was erected on a different alignment; at Glenlochar the second Flavian occupation seems to have covered the annexe of the first; at Castledykes the defences were recast; the small fort at Cappuck was enlarged and Oakwood was strengthened. Nowhere are these changes associated with evidence of disaster to the first structures. At Milton the first fort had been deliberately dismantled. Changes of such ubiquity and such extent are not merely what might have been coincident with the appointment of a new Governor, but are consistent with the substantial reduction of the British garrison around A.D. 87, which must have involved regrouping of forces on a drastic scale, if not a temporary abandonment.[1] The clue no doubt lies in the forts along the mountain margin in Perthshire, of which Fendoch alone has been excavated. But the excavation of Inchtuthil, now in progress, reveals the complete abandonment, systematically and deliberately undertaken, of the great legionary fortress, and with this must go the evacuation of other sites, like Fendoch, yet

[1] This would give point to the gibe of Tacitus in *Hist.* I, 2

to be discovered. For the little forts which succeeded the legionary fortress are associated with what appears to be a frontier barrier, namely the Cleaven Dyke. This earthwork consists of an earthen bank thirty feet wide at the base, flanked at some distance on either side by a shallow, flat-bottomed ditch which runs for some 3,000 yards across the approach to Inchtuthil from the north, where rivers form an awkward re-entrant. Its obvious relationship to these rivers and to Inchtuthil, and also the short extent of its course, indicate that it is a special local expedient, 'an artificial barrier, blazing through the forest the limits of Caesar's land.' [1] Eastwards towards the sea, however, there is nothing that could be construed as part of a frontier system. It is fairly clear, therefore, that in thinking of a frontier we should not here envisage a continuous barrier. Instead, we should think of the main road to Strathmore, with its associated forts and signal-stations, as itself constituting a *limes* by its deep penetration into barbarian territory. The road follows a course, intermittently known, from Camelon on the Isthmus, over the Forth near Stirling, to Ardoch and so to Strageath, on the Earn; from there it goes, lined by frequent signal-stations, to the fort of 'Bertha' at the junction of Almond and Tay. At one period in its history it continued north-eastwards to Cardean, some fourteen miles in advance of Inchtuthil, and although this is at the moment the northernmost permanent Roman fort known, we cannot assume that it represents the final limit of knowledge. Nor is it yet known whether Cardean is part of the Flavian system.

Even, however, if it is assumed that there was no further penetration than the later fort at Inchtuthil and the forts south-west of it at the mouths of the glens, the picture is tenuously unconvincing. The penetration into territory so recently and so fiercely hostile is at once weak and deep. During the Antonine period, when the same road came once more into similar use, the Antonine Wall served as a base, providing a reservoir of troops to draw upon in emergency and accommodation for storage of supplies. Moreover, the western

[1] Richmond, *PSAS* LXXIV (1939–40), 45

section of the Wall, running close to the outlying part of the Highland mass, represented by the Campsie and the Kilpatrick Hills, guarded against any attack from that quarter. In the Flavian period nothing is known of such salutary precautions. The road runs deep into the North from no clearly adequate base and with no protection on its dangerously exposed west flank. To meet part of the difficulty, the late Mr S. N. Miller suggested [1] that the western part of the Forth-Clyde line continued to be held in the post-Agricolan period, but if that is so, the structural remains seem elusive. It is thus clear that many points remain to be elucidated.

Nor is the detailed picture of the Roman occupation of southern Scotland in any sense complete. Even the main lines of the pattern, though clear, are still fragmentary. The two main northward routes, are reasonably clear, but of the two east-to-west roads, one apparently branches near Lockerbie from the Annandale road and, by way of Dalswinton on the Nith reaches the Dee at Glenlochar, about two miles north of Castle Douglas. From there, simple probability and an air-photograph of an apparently Roman site at Gatehouse-of-Fleet (not yet tested) would suggest that it reached the sea in the neighbourhood of Stranraer. The other, starting from Newstead, goes by Lyne on the Tweed to Castledykes and so to Loudoun Hill on the Ayrshire border. This once more suggests contact with the sea, somewhere in Irvine Bay. But no Flavian permanent site is yet securely attested north-west of Castledykes, and there is yet no trace of Flavian occupation of the area from middle and upper Nithsdale westwards, though the large size of the fort at Dalswinton indicates the importance attached to this front. Only at Glenlochar is a hint given, by a road which starts northwards up the valley, though its date within the Roman period and its destination are alike unknown. There is thus a prospect that a pattern in the West may in due course emerge.

Returning, however, from detail to the general picture, it may be emphasised that the occupation in its second phase

[1] *Roman Occupation of SW Scotland* (1952), 211–12

was clearly no ephemeral experiment, but was undertaken with determination and in force. For a period of twelve to fifteen years, the Roman administration usual in such areas had opportunity to function over Scotland up to and including Perthshire. What this meant to a native population has already been indicated, and it cannot be doubted that the usual requisitions of men and labour and produce were imposed, and that taxation had begun to be organised. It must be assumed that everywhere during those years the impact of Roman government upon native life was very real, and it is likely that from resentment born of that impact revolt finally came. There is no real evidence of what tribal organisation existed or of the effect of Roman administration upon it. Only at Traprain Law,[1] in the territory of the Votadini, is it known that an *oppidum* of size was existing when the Romans came and was permitted to continue, facts which argue a measure of collaboration in the tribe to which it belonged. The hill-fort of Dalry [2] in Ayrshire may also be noted. Others were dismantled, the newly built forts on the Borders,[3] for instance, and the great *oppidum* of the Selgovae overlooking Newstead. The strong forts built in Gallic style in the Abernethy area had perished, whether at Roman hands or not is uncertain: certainly no Roman relics occur in them.[4] Of this we may be sure, that no native centre of power was tolerated which seemed likely to become a focus of trouble.

Administration apart, these years saw the same beginnings of intercourse between native and Roman as has been described for the north of England. Annexes sprang up beside forts and throve. The famous report on Newstead still gives the fullest picture of that intercourse in all its variety. And though Newstead may have been exceptional, in that it may have been the administrative centre of a large area to which numbers of natives perforce came, yet elsewhere, as at Milton, there is clear

[1] A. O. Curle and Cree, *PSAS* LV (1920–1), 153–206; LVI (1921–2), 189–259; A. H. A. Hogg in *Aspects of Archaeology* (1951), 200–20

[2] Smith, *PSAS* LIII (1918–9), 124

[3] C. M. Piggot, *PSAS* LXXXIV (1949–50), 134

[4] V. G. Childe, *The Prehistory of Scotland* (1935), 194

evidence of the congregation of natives and their women-folk round military posts.[1] Some would come for official purposes and go; some would come to barter native products for the goods of civilisation (witness the oyster-shells at Newstead)[2]; some would come for employment and remain. Native women were present always, doubtless pursuing the ancient profession of their kind. They brought with them the combs and the weaving utensils of the western duns.[3] Altogether the picture resembles that of today when troops of a civilised power occupy posts in a barbarous land.

Beyond the immediate vicinity of the forts, Roman pottery found its way to the loch-dwellings of Galloway, to the caves of the Solway, to the earth-houses of Angus, to the hill-forts of Ayrshire, and as far beyond the occupied area as the Orkneys and the Outer Isles.[4] Such evidence speaks more of the coming and going of traders than of definite direct influence of the occupation. And the evidence of coins has a similar significance. The distribution maps show clearly that coins circulated not only from the hands of Roman troops but also in the course of trade, and that circulation was quite considerable. Miss Anne Robertson has recently underlined an earlier conclusion of Sir George Macdonald, that the quantity of first-century Roman coinage circulating in Scotland was at least as great as that associated with the much longer Antonine occupation.[5] The inventory drawn up by James Curle serves to show the widespread distribution of articles of metal and glass and of trinkets for personal adornment from Roman sources or from areas under more developed Roman rule.[6] Yet, impressive though such lists and inventories may seem, they lose some of their impressiveness when compared with similar records from areas such as East Prussia, where Rome never penetrated, but which nevertheless have a wider and more plentiful distribution of Roman coins and objects, even

[1] *Trans. Dum. & Gall. Ant. & Nat. Hist. Soc.* XXVIII (1949–50), 202

[2] J. Curle, *A Roman Frontier Post and its People* (1911), 118

[3] ibid. pl. LXVIII; see V. G. Childe, *Prehistoric Communities of the British Isles* (1940), 255

[4] J. Curle, *PSAS* LXVI (1931–2), 282–9

[5] *PSAS* LXXXIV (1949–50), 153

[6] ibid. LXVI (1931–2), 277–397

of the first century, than Scotland can show.[1] The difference is instructive, for East Prussia lay upon the amber route, and Scotland had no prized object of trade which attracted commerce to her depths. There is thus in Scotland no series of rich objects suggestive of cultural impact or valued trade richly recompensed. Indeed, the flat rotary quern, which now replaced the older bee-hive form, is perhaps the only real legacy of the occupation to the native life of the Scottish North.[2] Artistic impulses found expression outside the pale of Roman rule, for instance in the great spiral armlets of Aberdeenshire. In northern England, where artistic craftsmanship was well established, production continued, but inspiration slept until it awoke again to the glory of God in the Dark Ages.

The total picture is one of an overwhelming military domination, making no impression save by its demands and seeking as yet no end save frontier security. A time came later when the Border lands, by long association, began to understand the majesty of Rome ; when native children were taught the Roman letters in the barbarian huts of Traprain Law, and the Roman way of life came to be looked upon as an ideal in a disintegrating world. That story belongs to another part of this book. It is a matter for speculation whether an understanding and positive influence would have come sooner, had the first-century occupation settled down to run a peaceful course.

Agricola's peace, shorn of its supporting force, did not endure. Soon after the opening of the second century disaster came. Newstead, Oakwood, Dalswinton, Glenlochar, Castledykes and even Corbridge went up in flames.[3] There was not time to remove military equipment at Newstead.[4] At Milton,

[1] Olwen Brogan, *JRS* XXVI (1936), 215

[2] V. G. Childe, *The Prehistory of Scotland* (1935), 224

[3] Newstead, *PSAS* LXXXIV (1949–50), 11 ; Oakwood, *PSAS* LXXXVI (1951–2), 105 ; Dalswinton, publication forthcoming ; Glenlochar, *Trans. Dum. and Gall Ant. & Nat. Hist. Soc.* XXX (1951–2), 12 ; Castledykes, *JRS* XLII (1952), 88 ; Corbridge, *AA*[4] XXXI (1953), 219

[4] J. Curle, *A Roman Frontier Post and its People* (1911), 113–14

though there was apparently no disaster, the evacuation took place in headlong haste.[1]

Whatever happened, it is coupled with the appearance of Northerners at Torwoodlee Broch,[2] and by their speedy expulsion. Did the North rally again under the leadership of some unknown hero and sweep south with such speed and force that the Roman garrisons were taken by surprise? It seems incredible. Yet what is the alternative? On the whole this major incident of northern history remains at present unexplained. Much excavation remains to be done, especially of native sites, before we can hope to know the truth. Meantime we have the fact that the Romans evacuated southern Scotland pell-mell, and that the movement compelled the withdrawal of the frontier south of the Cheviot on lines not yet securely known. A generation later there was a serious war of which history and coinage alike speak. That war was raging when Hadrian became Emperor in A.D. 117, and its successful conclusion led to a visit of the Emperor himself and the building of the Wall between the Tyne and Solway which bears his name. We know nothing of that war, except that victory was at a price. The Ninth Legion, which had been in the front line of the fighting ever since the conquest, disappeared from the Army List, annihilated or disgracefully defeated, it has commonly been supposed, about this time.[3]

[1] *Trans. Dum. & Gall. Ant. & Nat. Hist. Soc.*, XXVIII (1949–50), 203

[2] S. Piggot, *PSAS* LXXXV (1950–1), 92–117

[3] For a recent discussion of the fate of the Ninth Legion see E. Birley, *Roman Britain and the Roman Army* (1953), 20–30. Recently, the question has arisen whether, in the years following A.D. 100, an attempt was made to hold a fringe of territory beyond the Tyne-Solway isthmus; but the matter is as yet undetermined archaeologically.

Chapter III

ROMAN AND NATIVE, A.D. 122–197

IMMEDIATELY before the period under review, which runs from A.D. 122, when the building of Hadrian's Wall was begun, to A.D. 197, when the legate of the Emperor Septimius Severus (A.D. 194–211) recovered the greater part of the province of Britain, there had been a serious setback to Roman arms. On the accession of the Emperor Hadrian (A.D. 117–138), Britain, we are told, was restive [1]; elsewhere we learn that in his reign many Roman soldiers lost their lives in Britain.[2] The details of the trouble at this time are obscure; and, excepting that, on the negative side, it is as certain as archaeological evidence can make it that Corbridge was not involved, its centre cannot be located. It is not known whether there was a revolt, or whether the province, whose boundary may have lain at this time either roughly on the line of the present Border, or already on the Tyne-Solway isthmus, was invaded from without.

There is nothing obscure about the steps taken to meet the situation. The massive and complicated system of fortifications, known collectively as Hadrian's Wall, was built between A.D. 122 and 128; it was constantly added to and modified until close on the end of the reign, in A.D. 138. It formed both an impregnable defensive system and a springboard for limited offensives or spoiling attacks.[3] However useful it may have proved incidentally, as a check on petty raiders or as a political and administrative boundary, its prime purpose was undoubtedly military. As Hadrian attempted to solve the problem he had inherited by building forward-facing defensive works, we have a hint of the direction from

[1] SHA, *Hadrian*, 5

[2] Fronto, *Epistulae* (ed. Naber, 1867), 218; Loeb edition, II, 22–3

[3] J. C. Bruce, *Handbook to the Roman Wall* (10th edn., 1947), 21

which the trouble of a few years before had come. Antiquaries who used to call the Wall 'The Picts' Wall' were nearer the truth than they knew. Further, the fact that in Hadrian's time outposts were held in the west, at Birrens, Netherby and Bewcastle,[1] while there is evidence that the outposts in the east, in Redesdale, were not yet established, suggests that any further offensive was expected to fall on the western sector.

In terms of the relations between Roman and Native, the Wall meant that there was a barrier, moral and legal as well as physical, between one group of British tribes and another. The people on either side of the frontier were in different worlds. The rigidity of the barrier may be illustrated from an incident on the Rhine, during the revolt of Civilis, about half a century earlier.[2] The Tencteri, a German tribe from the east bank of the Rhine, sent ambassadors to the citizens of Cologne, who, though Romanised and intermarried with citizens of other origin, were of the same stock as themselves. One of the complaints of the Tencteri was that they were cut off from their kinsmen on the west bank, and were only allowed to cross the Rhine un-armed, under guard, by day, at fixed points and times, and had to pay for the privilege. There was, however, a specially favoured German tribe on the Rhine-Danube frontier, the Hermunduri,[3] who, because of their past loyalty to Rome, alone of all the German tribes, were allowed the privilege of entering the province of Raetia for the purpose of trade, instead of being confined to the river bank. It is possible that a specially favoured tribe, or tribes, in the territory to the north of Hadrian's Wall, in treaty relationship with the Empire, might have been granted similar privileges; there is evidence to be considered which may indicate which particular tribe, or tribes, in northern Britain might have so qualified. But the general situation remains unaltered; it is summed up in these words by the only Roman

[1] E. Birley, *PSAS* LXXII (1937–8), 275–347 (Birrens); *CIL* VII, 961 (Netherby); *CIL* VII, 978 (Bewcastle)
[2] Tac. *Hist.* IV, 64
[3] Tac. *Germ.* 41

writer[1] who records the building of Hadrian's Wall: 'he built a Wall eighty miles long which was to divide the Romans from the barbarians.'

When our only written source describes the folk on either side of the Wall in different terms, it is expressing an intention rather than describing an actual situation. In practice, when it was first built, the Wall could justly be described as a 'barrier separating one set of hostile, un-Romanised barbarians from another.'[2] The remains of the Wall on the ground are themselves an illustration of the intention to treat the folk on either side differently. One of the modifications made to the Wall during its building was the construction, to the south of it, of the earthwork known as the Vallum; this consists essentially of a flat-bottomed ditch with symmetrically disposed upcast. While the Vallum was clearly southward-facing, in the sense that it runs on the southern side of the installations, and that the crossings opposite the milecastles were originally so arranged that the space between the ditch and the south mound could be patrolled by the milecastle garrisons, it is in no sense a southward-facing defence. In places it is extraordinarily badly sited for defence against the south; west of Housesteads, 'bar gunpowder, a party of schoolboys could stone the best troops in the world out of the Vallum.'[3] The symmetry of the work, its non-military nature, to which R. G. Collingwood[4] repeatedly drew attention, make it look as if it were deliberately designed to be unoffensive. Its function was clearly to prevent the access of unauthorised persons, which is not the same as hostile persons, to the Wall and its incorporated structures. The contrast between the Vallum and the Wall is parallel to the contrast in the Augustan History between Roman and barbarian.

At one point Wall and Vallum come into direct contact with a small native homestead. This is at Milking Gap,[5]

[1] SHA *Hadrian*, 11 [2] J. Morris, *CW*² L (1950), 43–53

[3] T. Hesketh Hodgson, quoted in *Handbook to the Roman Wall* (1947), 132

[4] R. G. Collingwood and J. N. L. Myres, *Roman Britain and the English Settlements* (2nd edn., 1937), 133

[5] H. E. Kilbride-Jones, *AA*⁴ xv (1938), 303–50

about a mile and a half west of Housesteads. A single group of stone-founded huts lies between the lines of the Wall and the Vallum. When it was excavated, many Roman or Romano-British objects were recovered. Except for one small fragment of pottery, described as Castor ware, which, if correctly diagnosed, is so far out of context that it may be dismissed at the outset as a probable stray from the nearby milecastle, the finds form an internally consistent group of the first or second quarter of the second century. The excavators, and the writers of the specialist reports, dated them to the time of Trajan and Hadrian, or a little later. Since then the suggestion has been made that the hamlet grew up in the reign of Antoninus Pius (A.D. 138–61), at the time when the frontier of the province was moved from the Tyne-Solway isthmus to the Forth-Clyde isthmus, about A.D. 140 ; at this time the Vallum was systematically breached at intervals along part of its length. If this explanation were correct, the settlement would provide an interesting case of land, which had been a prohibited military zone shortly before, being leased to native herdsmen or farmers.

A re-examination of the report, however, reveals that there is nothing that need be dated later than the middle of Hadrian's reign, and there is much that may be earlier. A dragonesque brooch, dated by Mr Kilbride-Jones to not later than A.D. 110, a fragment of decorated samian in the style of Medetus or Ranto of Vichy, and dated by the late Mr J. A. Stanfield to A.D. 110–15, and a group of coarse pottery, not one piece of which would look out of place at Throp or Haltwhistle Burn, are the most closely datable pieces. An alternative explanation of the Milking Gap settlement would then be that its life came to an end when the Vallum was dug in the middle of Hadrian's reign, and not that its life began when the Vallum was slighted at the beginning of the next reign. The picture is perhaps grimmer ; it is one of requisition rather than de-requisition.

The possibility that a state in treaty relationship with the Empire lay north of the Wall has already been mentioned.

If such a state existed at this time, though there is no direct evidence for it, we should look for it in the east. As we have already seen, the western end of the Wall caused more concern to Hadrian's legates than the eastern; it was in the west that outposts were held from the first, and it was there, at Stanwix, north of Carlisle, that the largest cavalry unit in Britain was stationed; it had been in the west for some thirty years or more, first at Dalswinton in Dumfriesshire, and then, possibly, at Carlisle itself. In the east, in the Lothians, Berwickshire, eastern Roxburghshire and Northumberland, were the Votadini; evidence to be considered makes it appear that they were traditionally allies of the province.

In A.D. 139, the year after Hadrian died, the fort at Corbridge, where the main road from York to the Firth of Forth crosses the Tyne, which had been kept on a care and maintenance basis for half a generation, was rebuilt by the Second Legion *Augusta*, when Antoninus Pius was Emperor and Lollius Urbicus Governor.[1] This signified a far-reaching change in the relations between Rome and the northern natives. For the second time a full-scale Roman invasion of Scotland was mounted. In one sense warfare is a relationship; it is the only relationship between Roman and Native about which the scanty literary sources provide much information. In a stricter sense warfare is not a relationship; from the Roman point of view the enemy had no legal rights; until terms were arranged he had to be ridden down and killed. This aspect of the relationship between Roman and Native is permanently depicted on two of the distance-slabs from the Antonine Wall.[2]

Archaeological traces of warfare which can be quite securely dated to this period are completely lacking. At the native hill-top town of Birrenswark,[3] with its Roman siege camps on either side, we may see, as it were frozen, a picture

[1] *JRS* XXVI (1936), 244

[2] G. Macdonald, *The Roman Wall in Scotland* (2nd edn., 1934), pls. III and LXIV

[3] D. Christison, J. Barbour and J. Anderson, *PSAS* XXXIII (1898–9), 198–249

of the kind of thing that probably happened; it is, however, almost completely certain that this episode belonged to a period other than about A.D. 140.

When the writer of the life of Antoninus Pius in the Augustan History refers briefly to the war fought in Britain by Lollius Urbicus, he uses the phrase *summotis barbaris*.[1] As Sir George Macdonald[2] and other scholars have pointed out, this seems to be an echo of the phrase used by Tacitus when referring to Julius Agricola's fourth campaign: *summotis velut in aliam insulam hostibus*. The enemy was pushed across the Forth-Clyde isthmus into what was virtually another island. In its Antonine context the phrase *summotis barbaris* may mean much the same; the hostile tribesmen were driven out beyond the isthmus to the mountain fastnesses whence they had emerged. The phrase was given quite another meaning by R. G. Collingwood, who took up an idea of E. Fabricius,[3] he interpreted it as referring to the transplantation of entire barbarian tribes from between Hadrian's Wall and the Antonine Wall to new homes on the Upper German frontier. The transplantation, he argued, resulted in the virtual depopulation of the eastern and central Lowlands and the southern Uplands. At least ten separate units, each known as a *numerus Brittonum*,[4] are attested by a large number of inscriptions, the earliest of which date from the time of Antoninus Pius, on the second line of a single long sector of the Upper German frontier. In the second century a *numerus* is a unit, distinguished from the regular *cohors*, raised among such peoples as Britons, Germans or Moors, on the borders of the Empire, or among such naturally combative hill-folk as the Raetians within it. It is generally accepted that the *numeri Brittonum* were raised from among tribesmen newly conquered by Lollius Urbicus. Some of the units bear subsidiary titles, such as Elantienses, Gurvedenses, Murrenses and Triputienses. These titles were derived from the names of rivers in the districts where the

[1] SHA *Antoninus Pius*, 5, 4
[2] Macdonald, op. cit. 49
[3] Collingwood and Myres, op. cit. 146
[4] G. L. Cheesman, *The Auxilia of the Roman Imperial Army* (1914), 86

units were stationed, and not brought with them from Britain. The use of local river names as unit subtitles, and the fact that the *numeri* were stationed for the most part on the old Upper German line, a dozen or so miles behind the new outer line, have been interpreted by German scholars[1] to mean that we are not dealing simply with military units. They regard the Brittones as communities of men, women and children, deported and resettled, between the old and the new lines, in the valleys from which the titles were taken; from amongst these, men fit for military service were organised into *numeri*, each under the command of a centurion from one of the legions in Germany, but, to judge from the style of the inscriptions, with subsidiary officers derived from the army in Britain. While this is convincing and may be accepted, there is no evidence that the scale of the deportation was such as to depopulate wide areas in Northern Britain, nor that the deportations were necessarily from between the two Walls, rather than from beyond the Antonine Wall. On the contrary, there is evidence that the newly occupied areas in Britain were not depopulated, for objects of second-century date, many of them specifically of early Antonine date, appear as thickly on non-military sites in the Lowlands and the southern Uplands as in any other part of Britain north of the Tyne-Solway isthmus (Map 5). Northern Britons were undoubtedly recruited and transferred to Germany; this was a normal fruit of victory, and there is direct evidence for this particular example of the practice. Depopulation is, however, quite another matter, and there is no convincing evidence for it.

The war ended with the establishment of a new frontier. In a sense, Hadrian's Wall had been a strategical failure, because the potential enemies to north and north-west were out of its reach; they could combine unmolested, and could overawe tribes whose inclination was towards peaceful co-

[1] W. Schleiermacher, 'Der obergermanische Limes und spätrömische Wehranlagen am Rhein,' *33 Bericht der römischen-germanischen Kommission, 1943–50*, (1951), 133–84

existence. Tactically the Wall had been so complete a success that it was decided to move the system, with modifications, bodily northwards. The aggressive campaign was fought, a victory was celebrated in A.D. 142, and the frontier was moved from Tyne-Solway to Forth-Clyde. There is not the slightest doubt that the frontier was moved. The Antonine Wall was not a mere breakwater in front of the still occupied Wall of Hadrian, and any estimate of the purpose of the Antonine Wall which is based on that assumption is inevitably deficient. On the old line small legionary detachments replaced the original fort garrisons, some of which were moved on to the new line, or into forts between the lines. The Vallum was slighted at close and regular intervals. The gates were removed from the milecastles, the pivot stones [1] being broken in the process, and free passage through the Wall was thus allowed at almost eighty points. The garrisons from the milecastles and turrets were probably employed to man the fortlets, of early Antonine date, each about twice the size of a milecastle, of which a considerable number have recently been discovered, or re-discovered, between the two Walls.

The new Wall, like the old, was the defended frontier of the province. The tribes behind it were now within the province, and their status had changed. How they were now treated would depend on their previous behaviour towards the Empire, just as at a much earlier date the treatment of the Regnenses of southern Britain had differed sharply from that accorded to their neighbours the Atrebates; the difference had depended on their different reactions to the Claudian invasion.

There was no rearward boundary dyke to the Antonine Wall. This was probably because there were less installations to protect from unauthorised approach; there were for instance, no milecastles or turrets. Even so, the absence of such a boundary, even more than the neutral character of the Hadrianic Vallum, emphasises the northward-facing character

[1] J. P. Gibson and F. G. Simpson, *CW*[2] XI (1911), 390–441; F. G. Simpson, *CW*[2] XIII (1913), 297–397; J. P. Gillam, *AA*[4] XXXI (1953), 165–74

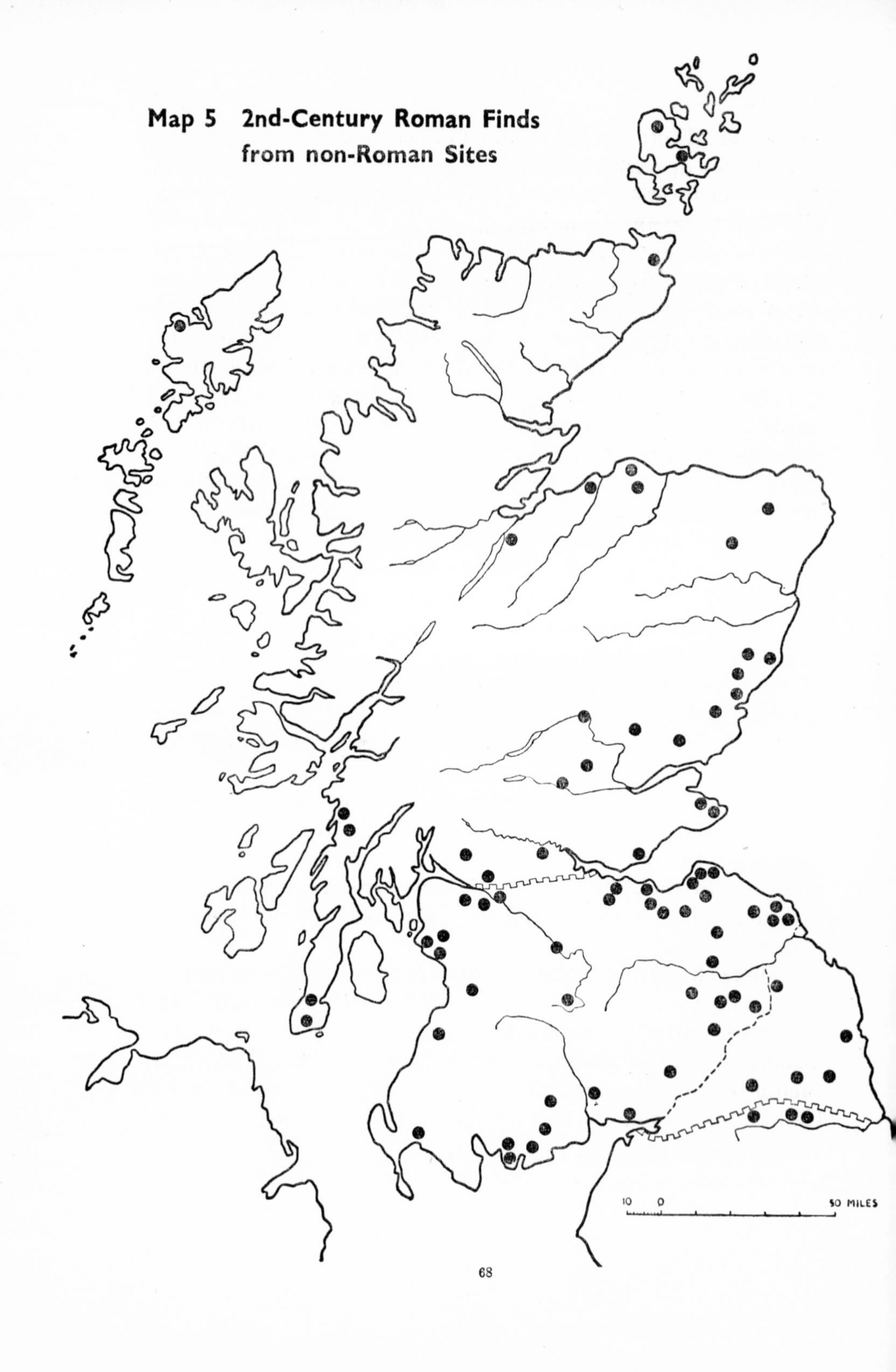
Map 5 2nd-Century Roman Finds
from non-Roman Sites
10 0
50 MILES

of the Antonine Wall ; the Novantae, Selgovae, Votadini and Damnonii, or a part of them, were now within the province.

The new Wall was less impressive than the old, but its forward ditch was more formidable, and its left flank was not ignored. In the event it was not a final success, but there can be little doubt that had it not been subject to strains that originated elsewhere, it could have effectively performed its function.

Map 5 shows the distribution of objects of second-century date found north of a line from Wearmouth to Carlisle, on other than Roman military sites. It has been prepared by abstracting from the late James Curle's inventory of objects of Roman or Roman provincial origin found in Scotland,[1] those which are quite certainly of second-century date. These are supplemented by contemporary objects found in Northumberland, or found in Scotland since Curle's list was published in 1932. Coins are included on the basic assumption that most second-century coins that are found will have been lost in the second century. Their distribution has been abstracted from Miss Anne Robertson's recently published tables of coin finds.[2] While the map cannot be claimed as completely accurate, either negatively or positively, the general picture that emerges is probably not misleading. A comparison between this map and the population map (Map 6), which is based on Professor Childe's distribution map of Iron-age monuments,[3] reveals the influence of other factors than mere density of population on the distribution of second-century objects. South of Aberdeen the two patterns are generally similar to each other, though they differ in detail. Where they correspond, the patterns on both maps are very similar to the pattern of distribution of arable land in recently published surveys of present-day land utilisation ; as it is hardly likely that finds made during cultivation will have grossly overweighted the pattern in certain areas, the correlation is

[1] *PSAS* LXVI (1931–2), 277–397
[2] *PSAS* LXXXIV (1949–50), 137–69
[3] V. G. Childe, *The Prehistory of Scotland* (1935), 275, Map IV

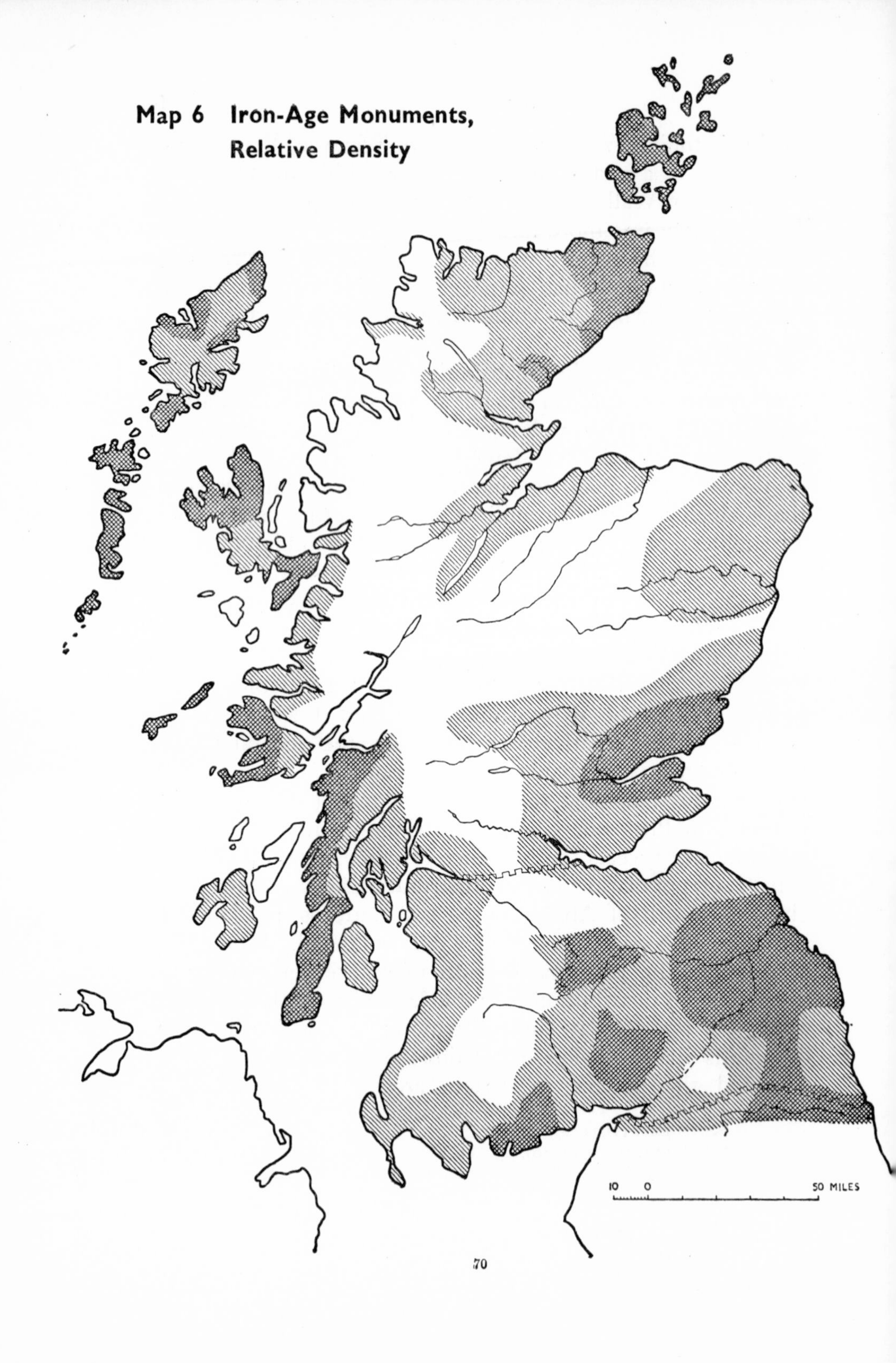
Map 6 Iron-Age Monuments,
Relative Density
10 0 50 MILES

doubtless due to fundamental geological factors affecting alike the Roman Iron Age and the present day. These fundamental factors influence all distribution maps of North Britain, either negatively or positively, and only the differences between various distributions are likely to be archaeologically significant. There is a striking difference between the distribution of second-century objects and the distribution of population in general. In the isles, in Argyll, and north of Aberdeen, second-century finds are scarce. Such objects as do appear are, as is to be expected, in the more populous regions, but, with inconsiderable exceptions, they are coastal, and are evidence only of coastwise sea-borne trade. The thickest clusters of finds are all either within the defended frontier, or in Fife and the more fertile parts of Perthshire and Angus, that is, in Strathmore, the Tay valley and Strathearn.

This concentration of finds in the region north of the eastern end of the Antonine Wall and south of Aberdeen is surely significant. The concentration stands out more sharply when Map 5 is compared with Map 7. This shows objects of first-century date found on non-Roman sites north of the present border between Scotland and England. It was prepared by Miss Anne Robertson, who has kindly allowed its use, from the same type of material as the second-century map. First-century finds are absent from that very region, north of the Tay, in which second-century finds cluster comparatively thickly. In fact, the finds seem to stop short at approximately the line of signal stations on the Gask ridge, which was probably the effective limit of the province, after the withdrawal of the legion from Inchtuthil, and before the disaster to Roman arms at the opening of the second century. When scattered objects from the far North and West are discounted, there is, then, a close correlation between the distribution of first-century objects and the extent of the province. If the distribution of second-century objects has anything like the same kind of significance, then it appears not unlikely that the region between the eastern end of the Antonine Wall and Aberdeen lay in some kind of special relationship to the

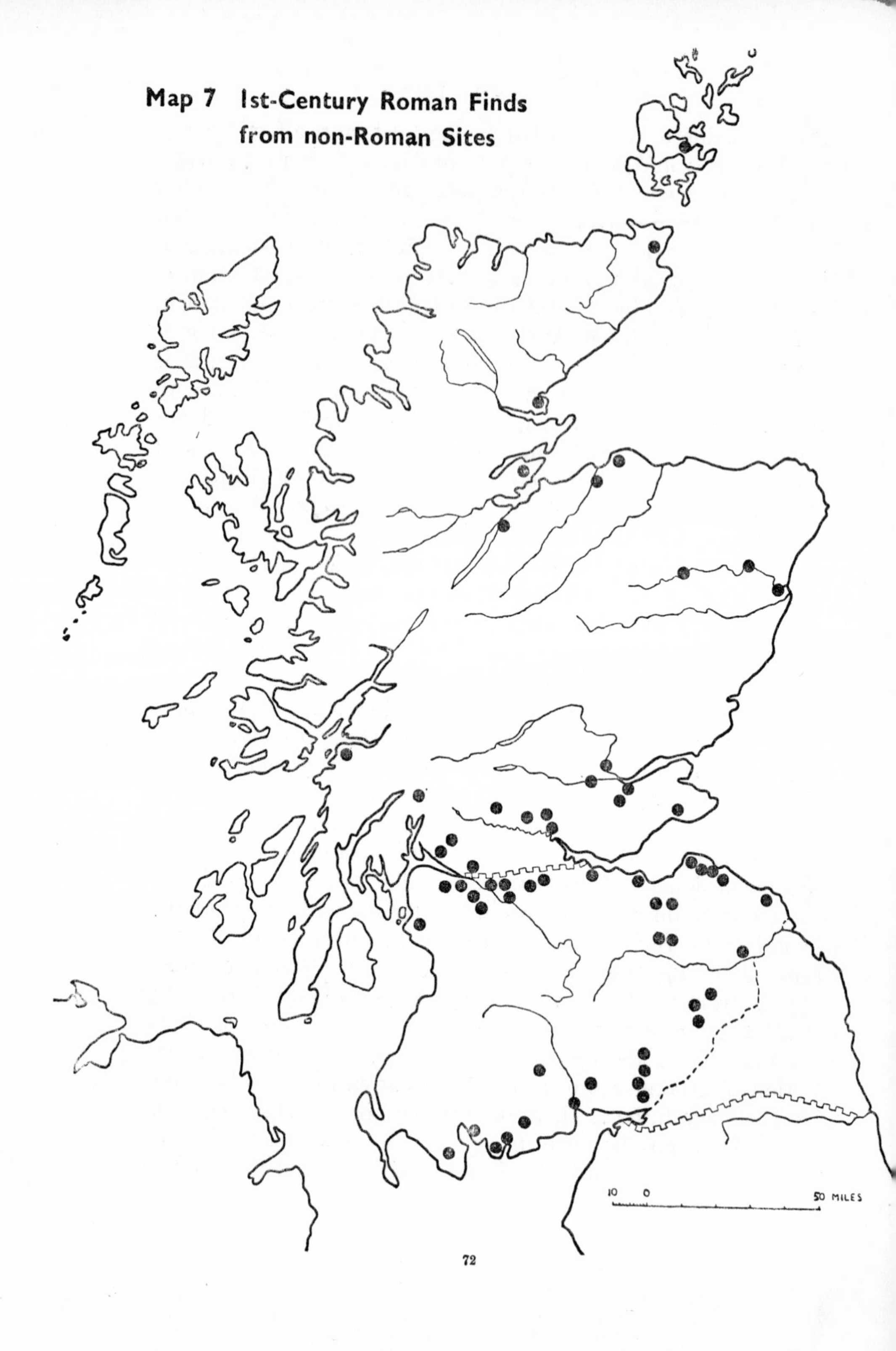
Map 7 Ist-Century Roman Finds
from non-Roman Sites
10 0
50 MILES

province in Antonine times. If this was in fact the case, it is to be expected that the tribes in this region would have been afforded some kind of military protection.

On Hadrian's Wall the outposts are in the west, to protect the Wall and its hinterland against hostile movements down Annandale, Eskdale and Liddesdale. The known outposts of the Antonine Wall, Ardoch, Dealginross, Strageath (which is a two-period site, one being not improbably Antonine) and Bertha, where there was undoubtedly Antonine occupation, are all in the east, and seem to be placed to protect the southern end of the fertile belt of country running through Perthshire against hostile irruptions down the glens from the hills to north and west. It is as though the people of the southern part of Strathmore, and of Fife, were being protected against their more warlike neighbours. Taken with the distribution of second-century objects, this implies that the southern part of Strathmore, and, with greater certainty, Fife, did in fact lie in some sort of special relationship to the province. The finds extend farther north, in the lower part of Angus, than any known Antonine military occupation. But if the fort at Cardean proved to be Antonine, then everything would fall into place. It seems to be a two-period site, and it would seem unlikely that, so far north, both should be Flavian, but, with the warning example of Inchtuthil in front of us, it would be unwise to go further than this.

On general grounds there are few sites north of the Antonine Wall where an Antonine outpost would have seemed more likely than Inchtuthil. A site chosen for a legionary fortress by Julius Agricola would, it seems at first sight, almost certainly have been chosen for a fort by Lollius Urbicus, who far more frequently planted his new forts on, or closely adjacent to, the sites of abandoned Agricolan forts, than at some distance from them. Yet, it is as certain as negative evidence can make it, that there was no Antonine occupation at Inchtuthil. There are structures to the east of the Agricolan fortress, which were excavated in 1901; they are parts of two successive forts, and are usually described as cohort-forts, though they may in fact have held detachments of legionaries. The pottery found during the excavations is preserved in the National Museum of Antiquities of Scotland. Every piece has been examined, and not one is certainly Antonine; nearly all are certainly and obviously Flavian; the few which are either unusual or undistinguished could well be Flavian, and are certainly not distinctively Antonine. This Inchtuthil pottery contrasts sharply with that from Ardoch, among which more than half the pieces are indubitably Antonine. But, although Inchtuthil legionary fortress is Flavian, it is unlikely that many of the pieces in question came from it, since the excavations of 1901 concentrated upon the area of the cohort-forts. Had either of these, then, been Antonine, pottery of this period could not have failed to have been present in the collection. The situation is, therefore, that at present evidence from native sites suggests more strongly than evidence from Roman sites, that Strathmore and Fife formed some kind of protectorate in the Antonine period. Such an arrangement would be to the mutual benefit of both the tribes and the Roman army; for while one party gained protection, the other gained control of the cultivable land to north and south of the lower Tay.

The Roman army may well have gained very considerable political and military advantages from the arrangement. The two tribes, or confederations of tribes, that were eventually responsible for the destruction of the second-century frontier systems, were the Maeatae, who lived near to the Antonine Wall, and the Caledonii, who lived beyond them. The southern frontiers of the tribes that gave their names to the coalitions were respectively on the upper Forth, where the name of a hill-fort, Dumyat, preserves the name of the Maeatae, and the regional name Fortrinn preserves that of their successors, the Verturiones, and in the upper Tay, where the place-names Schiehallion, Rohallion and Dunkeld preserve the name of the Caledonii.[1] Two points that emerge from the account of the warfare at the close of the second century and at the beginning

[1] F. T. Wainwright, *The Problem of the Picts* (1955), 52

of the third, are that the Caledonii and Maeatae were not always capable of concerted action, and that the Maeatae were regarded by the Romans as having broken faith. The protectorate system that has been envisaged would effectively cut off the Caledonii and Maeatae from each other, and enable feelings of loyalty to the Roman Empire to be fostered among the Maeatae. The statement by Dio, that treaties were broken,[1] suggests that the Maeatae may have been in treaty relationship with the Empire in Antonine times. This system of playing off tribe against tribe was an old and well-tried part of Roman statecraft, and one that was in fact used in the Antonine period on the Danube. It does not seem to have been unsuccessful in Britain, so long as there were sufficient Roman troops to stiffen the Maeatae and save them from being coerced into alliance with the Caledonii. If the extent of the protectorate is indicated with any accuracy by the pattern of second-century finds, then this might show which of the tribes named by Ptolemy went to make up the coalition to which the Maeatae gave their name. It would seem, for instance, that, among others, it would include the Venicones of Strathmore.

Whether or not folk as far north as Angus were under Roman control in the Antonine period, as the folk of Cheviot were to be in the third century ; whether, in other words, the provincial boundary was thought of as running along the edge of the Highlands, and out to sea just south of Aberdeen, or as running along the Antonine Wall, the peoples south of that Wall were in any case within the province. South of the Antonine Wall, the comparative rarity of second-century finds in Wigtownshire and Kirkcudbrightshire is striking. As the region is not empty of Iron-Age monuments, the scarcity of Roman objects may mean that the inhabitants, the Novantae, while undoubtedly within the province, had little contact with Rome ; they were probably not philo-Roman. The care with which Hadrian protected the Cumberland coast with a continuous regular chain of mile-fortlets and towers, the

[1] Dio, LXXV, 5, 4

maintenance of the western outposts, and the planting of the thousand strong *ala Petriana* towards the western end of the Wall, are all in part explained if the Novantae were inclined to be hostile. By contrast, objects cluster thickly in the land of the Damnonii. Again, the valleys of the Yarrow and the upper Tweed contrast sharply with the areas immediately to north and north-east ; here a difference between the attitude of the Selgovae of the centre and the Votadini of the east towards the government may be detected.

The difference in status between the Selgovae and the Votadini is reflected in the difference between Bonchester and Traprain Law. The hill-fortress of Bonchester, Roxburghshire, like the Roman fort of Newstead, Trimontium, was almost certainly in the territory of the Selgovae. No Roman objects of any kind were discovered during the excavations there.[1] By contrast, at Traprain Law, in East Lothian, in the territory of the Votadini, Roman objects, of all periods, and of the Antonine period in particular, are more abundant than on any other native site. The broch at Torwoodlee on the Gala Water is in piquant contrast to both these sites.[2] It was evidently dismantled by the Roman army. The Roman pottery used by the natives before the dismantling was, as Dr Steer points out, all pre-Hadrianic, and probably Flavian, however obtained. Dr D. B. Harden considered that colourless glass found there was of second-century date. It is clear that Torwoodlee had almost certainly gone by the time the area again formed part of the province, whether it was dismantled by the troops who early in the second century removed the dead and cleared the destroyed fort at Newstead, or by those operating in Scotland either early in Hadrian's reign or under Lollius Urbicus. While the site is in the land of the Selgovae, the builders were doubtless intruders from the far north. The Selgovae themselves were treated no differently ; Roman signal stations were planted on the sites of hill fortresses on Ruberslaw and on the North Eildon.

[1] C. M. Piggott, *PSAS* LXXXIV (1949–50), 113–36
[2] S. Piggott, *PSAS* LXXXV (1950–1), 92–117

The situation at Traprain Law[1] was vastly different. Whether or not it was the *curia* of the Votadini, we may almost claim for it the status of capital of a client kingdom. Second-century coins, and second-century pottery, imported from other parts of the province and from farther afield, have been found in some abundance. To take two examples: figured samian ware from central Gaul, some stamped by the potter Cinnamus, and other pieces in the style of Cinnamus, Advocisus, and the so-called 'potter of the small **S**', all Antonine potters, appears on the site; while coarse pottery of common provincial types, quite different from the native pottery, and securely datable to the Antonine period, is also abundant. Undoubtedly there was north-bound trade, for we are not dealing here, as perhaps in the earth-houses or at Torwoodlee, with vessels salvaged from deserted Roman forts.

The inhabitants of Traprain Law purchased their best pottery, ultimately, from factories at a great distance. Their worst pottery was almost indescribably bad. A pottery industry, in any real sense, can hardly be said to exist. Many fragments of native pottery were discovered in the course of the excavations. It was hand-made, coarse, often soft, and, when hard, full of grit or pitted with holes left by grit dissolved in the soil. The forms of pottery found at Traprain Law have no close cultural connections; because some of the forms are so simple that they have too many parallels, few of them are significant. A strong hint of Iron-Age A influence can be detected in some of the pieces; others are clearly imitations of Romano-British coarse pottery vessels. The Romano-British vessels which served as models were themselves derived from types of the pre-Roman Iron Age in the south of England, but as the styles reached Traprain Law at second hand they cannot be used as evidence for the cultural connections of the Votadini. The contrast between Votadinian pottery and Glastonbury pottery could hardly be more

[1] A. O. Curle, *PSAS* XLIX (1914–15), 139–202 (Traprain Law); further reports in *PSAS* L, LIX, LV, LVI, LVII, LVIII and LXXIV

complete; in this respect, as will appear, the pottery appears to tell a different story from the metal-work.

Votadinian pottery was home-made, for home use, and it hardly ever appears on a Roman military site. The situation was quite different in southern England when that was newly conquered. There the native communities were not only self-supporting for pottery supplies, but were able to supply pottery to the Roman army, in their own styles, and in rapidly improving techniques. The army was thus enabled to live off the country for much of its pottery, in a way that it was at first unable to do in northern England, and was never able to do in Scotland. When we turn to the Roman-period native villages of Yorkshire, in particular of Wharfedale, though the point applies to caves, farms and villages throughout the dales, there seems at first sight to be the same contrast between Roman and native wares as at Traprain Law. Further study reveals, however, that the native wares of central and western Yorkshire, like the calcite-gritted wares of eastern Yorkshire, which they closely resemble, are not only technically superior to the Votadinian wares, but also that they occur in large quantities on Roman sites. The native pottery of the Yorkshire dales appears not only in caves, villages and un-Romanised farms, but also in fortresses, forts, towns and villas. This state of affairs had already begun by the second century, but it reached its peak in the third and fourth centuries, by which time generations of the Brigantes had grown up on the Roman side of Hadrian's Wall, and the tribe had been fully assimilated into the province, albeit in a different way from the tribes of southern England. Brigantian pottery was made by professionals for the market, and was sold to rich and poor, townsman and countryman, soldier and civilian. Votadinian pottery, by contrast, was thought to have been made, as in primitive communities the world over, by the women of the tribe for their own use. The assimilation of the Votadini had not proceeded so far as that of the Brigantes, even in the second century. In the northern part of the Antonine province the blurring of the boundary between Roman and Native that is found increasingly farther south, had not begun. The Votadini obtained some pottery from provincial sources, but there seems to have been no common market for troops and civilians. The Antonine garrisons in Scotland obtained none of their pottery from sources nearer than the Stanegate, and much of it from still farther afield.

While pottery usefully indicates the degree of Romanisation, it is necessary to look away from pottery for evidence of the cultural connections and technical achievement of the people who lived on Traprain Law. Among the finds made there are portions of two-piece clay moulds for making small bronze articles, including a ring-headed pin, and a so-called dress-fastener. The dress-fastener consists of a bronze button with a pierced triangular shank; the shank springs from the centre of the back, is bent over at right angles into a plane parallel with the button, and projects well beyond its edge. It has been suggested that the object was a harness fitting; one or two have been found along with undoubted harness fittings, and the shank is often, though not always, well adapted to take a strap. It is, however, difficult to explain all the examples in this way, and the function of the object is probably correctly described by the term 'dress-fastener.' The bent and pierced shank could be sewn, out of sight, behind the edge of a garment, or a small strap or cord could be passed through it and fastened back on itself. As no complementary metal loop seems to have been found, the head of the fastener was presumably slipped into a looped cord or slit strap on the other edge of the garment.

There are many different types of dress-fastener, but four distinctive types stand out; the others are either represented by single examples only, or are clearly variants of one of the other four. The four types (Fig. 1) are (*a*) double-headed, (*b*) petal-headed, (*c*) disk-headed, and (*d*) square-headed.

The double-headed dress-fastener (Fig. 1, A) is the earliest. It appears, more than once, at Glastonbury, at Lydney, where it was assigned to the Iron Age and not to the late-Roman

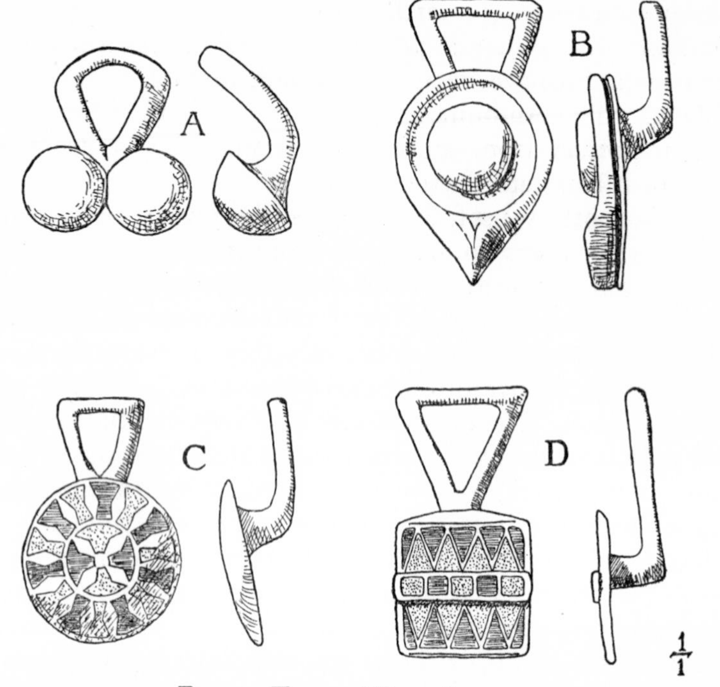

FIG. 1 Types of Dress Fastener

occupation, at Lakenheath in Suffolk, where it was dated to the first century of the present era, and at the Roman fort of Brough-under-Stainmore, which is a Flavian foundation. It has not been recorded in Scotland, though a fastener from Lochspouts crannog incorporates a pair of rounded bosses in its otherwise unique design. The double-headed type thus belongs to the pre-Roman Iron Age, but lasted until the last quarter of the first century.

The petal-headed dress-fastener (Fig. 1, B) comes next. Two identical fasteners of this type form part of the hoard of Iron-Age metal-work, mainly harness fittings, from Middlebie in Dumfriesshire. Two were found in Flavian contexts at Newstead; most of the others have been found on such Roman sites as Brough, Corbridge, Wroxeter and York, which were occupied in the Flavian period, and there appear to be no examples of the type from the forts on Hadrian's Wall, though fasteners of other types appear. The petal-headed type thus belongs, in the main, to the later first century, but may have lasted until the early years of the second.

The earliest disk-headed fastener (Fig. 1, C) comes from the Roman fort of Slack, in the West Riding; here it is almost certainly earlier, though not necessarily much earlier, than the beginning of the reign of Antoninus Pius. The type appears at Chesters, on Hadrian's Wall, where it can hardly be pre-Hadrianic, and may be later, at Newstead, Corbridge, Mumrills and High Rochester, among other sites which were occupied in the Antonine period, and at Caerleon, possibly as a survival, in a deposit of the third or fourth century. The disk-headed type may thus be provisionally assigned to the Hadrianic-Antonine period, though it may have survived as a type for an indefinite length of time after this.

The square-headed fastener (Fig. 1, D) resembles the disk-headed fastener closely, and it is probably roughly contemporary with it. It is commonest at Traprain Law, and it is found on such other sites as Chesters and Corbridge, which were occupied in the Antonine period.

In a list of 80 specimens of dress-fasteners of various types, from 29 different places, a list which, while by no means exhaustive, is probably representative, 26 come from Traprain Law, 8 from other native contexts in Scotland, 33 from Roman military stations in Scotland or northern or western England, 7 from pre-Roman Iron-Age contexts in southern England, 5 from large Roman towns in England, 1 from a Roman site of unknown character in England, and none from villas. While the figures are probably neither large enough in themselves, nor complete enough for confident statistical analysis, they tend to suggest that the dress-fastener was not part of the normal equipment of the land-owning class, and only to a limited extent part of that of the town-dweller. The frontier garrisons were doubtless in intimate contact with the un-Romanised natives of the North and West, and it is these folk whose clothes were fastened with these objects.

Most of the square and disk-headed fasteners are decorated with coloured enamel inlays ; some are in three colours, red, yellow and blue, and many are in two. They serve to remind us of the gay touches apparent in the dress of the British peasant in the Roman period. The dress-fastener thus falls into place in the cultural framework. It is Romano-British rather than merely Roman or merely British. It is at home within the province, but also in the less Romanised regions. When it appears at Drumashie, beyond the farthest limits of permanent Roman penetration, it carries a sense of Rome ; when it appears at the Roman chartered town of Colchester it carries a sense of the Celtic north ; at Traprain Law it is at home. The dress-fastener falls into the same social and economic level, the same Roman-period peasant culture, as the bone weaving comb, the bone toggle, the flattened beehive type of quern, the ring-headed bronze pin and the spiral bronze ring. The origin and the generalised ultimate distribution of these classes of object is similar, though there is a difference in detail. While the various objects, taken together, typify the Roman-period peasant culture of the north of Britain, a distinction has to be made between the utilitarian stone and bone instruments, and the metal objects of personal adornment. The distribution of weaving combs, bone toggles and the particular type of quern links south-western England, not only with south-eastern Scotland and the Atlantic coast, but also with the north of England. The distribution of ring-headed pins and spiral rings [1] seems to provide a direct link between Scotland and south-western England, without including the north of England.

The dress-fastener, too, is without doubt in the south-western English Iron-Age B cultural tradition. Three fasteners were found at Glastonbury, and single ones have come from Iron-Age contexts in Gloucestershire, Berkshire, Norfolk and Suffolk. The remainder of the pattern of distribution (Map 8) is a familiar one ; when the five pre-Roman English sites are discounted, all but two of the places of discovery fall north

[1] C. M. Piggott, *PSAS* LXXXIV (1949–50), 132

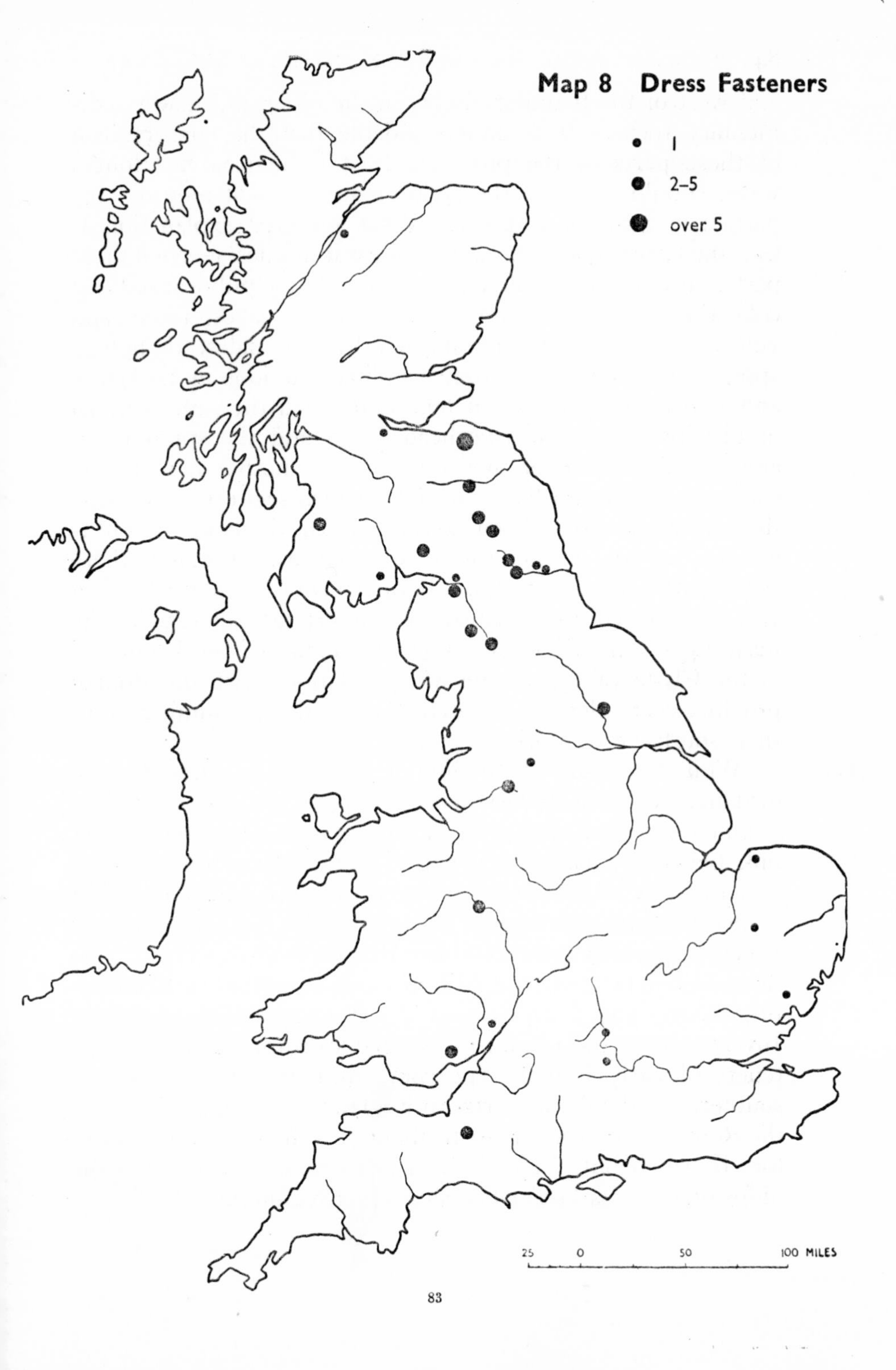
Map 8 Dress Fasteners
1
2–5
over 5
25
0
50
100 MILES

and west of the boundary between the older and newer sedimentary rocks. It is understandable that the conservatism of these parts of the province, least influenced by Roman ways, should preserve the style of dress which required the particular form of fastener. What requires explanation is how the fastener, and the style of dress it implies, reached these parts. It is absent, so far as a scanning both of publications and collections has so far revealed, from the caves, farms and villages of the Yorkshire and Derbyshire dales, though it appears occasionally on Roman military stations in Yorkshire and Lancashire. In fact it falls into much the same pattern of distribution as the ring-headed pin and the spiral ring; and the dress-fastener may thus be yet another item in the short but significant list of artefacts which seem to have made their way, as types, from south-western England to south-eastern Scotland without intermediate stages. If so, then there can be little doubt that the folk of the south-western English Iron-Age B culture formed an important element in the make-up of the Votadini. The very name of the Damnonii of the Clyde valley, a tribe whose relations with the Roman province seem closely to match those of the Votadini, betrays their south-western origin.

While the result of this line of argument is attractive, the evidence of the dress-fasteners is perhaps too slender to lend it much support. Other explanations of the apparent direct link between Glastonbury and Traprain Law are possible. The majority of the dress-fasteners from Traprain Law are of Hadrianic-Antonine type; comparatively few are of early Roman type, and none are of pre-Roman Iron-Age type. The dress-fasteners from the Milton Loch crannog in Kirkcudbrightshire, and from beyond the frontier at Drumashie in Inverness-shire, are again of Hadrianic-Antonine type. Fasteners of early Roman type come from military stations in southern Scotland and northern England. The possibility that the Roman army was the instrument of diffusion cannot therefore be ruled out. The Roman army may have assisted the diffusion of dress-fasteners over a wider region than the British province. Three examples of enamelled disk-headed fasteners are known from the province of Pannonia.[1] As British *auxilia* were stationed in Pannonia, and as Pannonian *auxilia* were stationed in Britain, particular specimens of dress-fasteners may have been carried in either direction.

The Roman roads, however, probably did as much to open up trade and to break down cultural boundaries as did the railways in the last century. They would make their own particular contribution to the spread of that Celtic, or Iron-Age B, cultural tradition which was the common heritage of the less Romanised provincials, and was an undertone to so much, within and without the province.

The fact that dress-fasteners of Hadrianic-Antonine type were made at Traprain Law, and that similar fasteners are found farther south, does not mean that non-ferrous metal products were objects of trade from north to south.

It has, however, been suggested 'that natives exchanged their local iron for pottery, glass, and other trade goods,' [2] for a smelting furnace for iron was discovered in Constantine's cave on Fifeness. This site is within the area which may have been under some sort of Roman protection, and the cave was certainly occupied in the Antonine period, for, among other Roman objects, an amphora was found there with the Antonine stamp P M S A. There is no proof that the inhabitants worked the local iron for sale rather than for their own use, or that their supplies of provincial goods were obtained in exchange for iron rather than for other natural products. On the other hand, a large ingot, made up of small blooms of iron hammered together, has been found at Corbridge. It was probably built up, in the third century, from blooms produced in Redesdale, in the outpost area of Hadrian's Wall. It is a possibility, though no more, that a similar use was made, in the second century, of the mineral products of the outpost area of the Antonine Wall.

[1] I. Sellye, 'Les Bronzes Émaillés de la Pannonie Romaine,' *Dissertationes Pannonicae*, Ser. 2, Fasc. 8 (1939), pl. VII, nos. 3, 4 and 5

[2] A. J. B. Wace and T. J. Jehu, *PSAS* XLIX (1914–15), 233–55

The gradual assimilation of the tribes south of Hadrian's Wall into provincial life has been remarked upon in connection with the pottery. Another symptom of the tendency is the growth of extra-mural settlements round Roman forts. Here again there is a contrast between the status of the natives of the province as extended by Antoninus Pius, and that of provincials of longer standing. The extra-mural settlement flourished in England in the third and fourth centuries, but there is much evidence that many were already established by the second century. At Little Chester [1] in Derbyshire, and at Malton in Yorkshire, extra-mural communities were flourishing by the Antonine period. Even farther north, well into the hill country, the impressive extra-mural settlements at Brough and Kirkby Thore in Westmorland,[2] have yielded evidence that they were already in existence in Antonine times; not least among the items of evidence is that the manufacture of small bronze brooches, harness trappings and other *objets d'art*, reached its peak at both these places in the Antonine period. At Corbridge, now that the limits of the Antonine fort underlying the visible remains are beginning to emerge, it is clear that many of the buildings on the outskirts of the site, which yielded Antonine objects when they were excavated before 1914, formed part of an extra-mural settlement.

On the other hand, on the line of Hadrian's Wall the picture is different. There is no positive evidence for second-century civil settlements, predecessors of those that lapped around the forts, and over the line of the Vallum, at a later date. It is clear, in fact, that within the Wall-Vallum zone they were at first actively discouraged. There is no very definite evidence for early settlements immediately south of the Vallum. North of Hadrian's Wall, and on the Antonine Wall, many of the forts have annexes. In plan they appear to be part of the military lay-out, and not infrequently contain the bath-house. At Newstead excavation revealed an annexe literally pitted with shafts for the disposal of purely military rubbish. While the third-century developments in England

[1] *JRS* XVI (1926), 222 [2] RCHM *Westmorland* (1936), xxxix

Plate 1 Trajan's Column: battle scene, with Roman auxiliaries fighting, one carrying a severed head with his teeth

Plate 2 Trajan's Column: firing of native dwellings, with Dacians in flight and Dacian fortifications, with captive heads exposed on poles in the background

Plate 3 Trajan's Column : a concentration camp for Dacian prisoners

Plate 4 Trajan's Column: surrender of Dacians in A.D. 102, with demolition of fortifications and whispering chiefs

Objects excavated at Newstead (Trimontium) in the Eildon Hills, Roxburghshire: (*above*) Roman helmets and visor-masks, dragonesque brooch, bronze buckle; (*left*) horn pin; (*below*) the Eildon Hills from Bemersyde

Llyn Cerrig chariot model

Tombstone of Salmanes

Left-hand relief of Bridgeness slab, showing a Roman victory over the Caledonians

Bewcastle silver plaque, showing Cocidius with a spear with knobbed end

Murrell Hill tombstone, showing lady with her child and a fan

Central Hut in second-century native settlement at Milking Gap, Northumberland

Plate 8

Customs gateway through Hadrian's Wall at the Knag Burn

Birdoswald, later fourth-century masonry at south gate

reveal other factors at work, the earliest extra-mural settlements there probably resembled the soldiers' bazaars outside the cantonments of British India. Forts in Scotland seem quite often to have reached the latter stage, but the history of the frontier was too disturbed for economic development to take deep root and flourish. The natives had little to offer; it is true that their own settlements are mainly on the most fertile land, and that the quern is as much a type fossil of the northern Iron Age as is the weaving comb, but both agriculture and horticulture were nevertheless at an extremely primitive stage. The Antonine occupation was of too brief duration for the creation of a potential new market to bring about far-reaching changes. In time such changes would doubtless have come. The distinction between Roman and Native would have largely disappeared, and a Romano-British community life would probably have developed; it would have resembled that of Brigantia rather than that of the south of England. As things were, political and military circumstances prevented the development.

The system of frontier control devised by Antoninus Pius and Lollius Urbicus was intended to meet the danger from the North. This danger had been ever present since the legion had been withdrawn from Inchtuthil. The method adopted was to include a greater number of barbarian tribes within the province; they were watched over by garrisons, loyalty being fostered and rewarded, disloyalty being checked and punished. The system was ultimately a failure; this was not because it was ill-conceived, nor was it because the frontier Wall and its outposts, which divided the new 'Romans' from the barbarians, was too weakly built to stand the strain. The failure was due to the fact that in addition to the troops on the line of the Wall, garrisons were required to do the work of maintaining loyalties throughout most of the country between the Trent and Strathmore. Relative to the size of the province, the garrison of Britain was the largest in the Empire, but spread out so thinly, it was barely equal to its task, and strains developed behind the Wall.

In A.D. 155 an insurrection had to be suppressed by the Governor Julius Verus. The only Roman fort known to have been destroyed in this rising is Birrens; it was rebuilt in A.D. 158. It is significant that, however wide an area was affected, south-west Scotland was involved. If, as seems likely, the siege of Birrenswark took place in actual warfare, and not in manoeuvres, it was possibly on this occasion. Unambiguous surface indications, confirmed by excavation in 1898, make it clear that the siege camp on the southern side of the fortress was constructed after a fortlet that lies at its north-east angle. As the fortlet is very similar in its layout and dimensions to the well-known series of early-Antonine fortlets, such as Dalmakethar or Durisdeer, and as pottery from the site, recently examined by Dr Steer, is Antonine, it is certain that the siege took place after the time of Lollius Urbicus.

In the years following the outbreak, and in particular early in the reign of Marcus Aurelius (A.D. 161–80), when Calpurnius Agricola was Governor, changes in frontier policy are implied by changes in the disposition of garrisons in the north of England, including the line of Hadrian's Wall.[1] Their precise scope and significance is not yet clear.

Early in the reign of Commodus (A.D. 180–93) the province was once more disastrously invaded from the North. The situation was recovered under the able leadership of the hard-bitten and experienced commander Ulpius Marcellus. Following this, at some date not as yet completely certain, the Antonine system was finally abandoned. In the third century a quite different solution of the frontier problem was attempted. Before this, in A.D. 196 or 197, the Caledonii combined with the Maeatae in breaking their treaties during the absence of the greater part of the Roman army from Britain, and swept, destroying as they went, as far south as York. With this invasion the second period of Roman influence in Scotland closed.

All that was left was a tradition of loyalty to Rome among

[1] J. P. Gillam, *Trans. Architec. & Arch. Soc. Durham & N'b'land* x pt. iv (1953), 359–75

the Votadini and the Damnonii, a dim foreshadowing of Gododdin and Strathclyde. For the rest the position may be summed up in the words of James Curle[1]: 'The Roman occupation of Caledonia was never very secure, nor was it of long duration. No towns sprang up under its shelter. The villas and farms common in southern Britain are absent.'

[1] J. Curle, op. cit. 277

Appendix

Alphabetical list of sites and counties where dress-fasteners have been found

	Site	County	
1	Benwell	Northumberland	1
2	Brough-under-Stainmore	Westmorland	2
3	Caerleon	Monmouthshire	2
4	Carlisle	Cumberland	2
5	Chapel House	Northumberland	1
6	Chesters	Northumberland	4
7	Colchester	Essex	1
8	Corbridge	Northumberland	5
9	Drumashie	Inverness-shire	1
10	Edgerston	Roxburghshire	2
11	Glastonbury	Somerset	3
12	Hagbourne Hill	Berkshire	1
13	High Rochester	Northumberland	2
14	Kidlington	Oxfordshire	1
15	Kirkby Thore	Westmorland	2
16	Lakenheath	Suffolk	1
17	Lochspouts	Ayrshire	2
18	Lydney	Gloucestershire	1
19	Manchester	Lancashire	3
20	Middlebie	Dumfriesshire	2
21	Milton Loch, Stewartry of	Kirkcudbright	1
22	Mumrills	Stirlingshire	1
23	Newstead	Roxburghshire	3
24	Ringstead	Norfolk	1
25	Slack	Yorkshire	1
26	Stanwix	Cumberland	1
27	Traprain Law	East Lothian	26
28	Wroxeter	Shropshire	4
29	York	Yorkshire	3
			80

Chapter IV

ROMAN AND NATIVE IN NORTH BRITAIN: THE SEVERAN REORGANISATION

IN A.D. 196 the Governor of Britain, Clodius Albinus, transferred the bulk of the Roman garrison of the province to the Continent in an unsuccessful attempt to wrest the imperial power from Septimius Severus, and on his defeat the northern tribes eagerly accepted the unexpected opportunity to break into the defenceless province. It is not yet certain whether the Antonine Wall was overthrown at this time, or whether, as Macdonald believed, it had already been relinquished, and its defences perhaps peacefully dismantled, some ten years earlier [1]; but tremendous havoc was wrought by the invaders on Hadrian's Wall, where forts, milecastles and turrets were systematically wrecked, while on the eastern flank the trail of devastation has been traced as far south as York.[2] As soon as Severus had consolidated his position, by defeating Albinus at Lyons in 197, one of his first acts was therefore to dispatch reinforcements to Britain, and to charge a new Governor, Virius Lupus, with the formidable task of retrieving the situation. And to ensure that no Governor in Britain would be strong enough to imitate Albinus, Severus divided the country into two provinces, Upper and Lower Britain, and placed each of them under a separate command.

[1] G. Macdonald, *The Roman Wall in Scotland* (1934), 479–82. The former alternative wins support from the fact that certain stamped *mortaria* which occur in the destruction deposits of 197 at Corbridge, are also found on the Antonine Wall (see J. P. Gillam, *Trans. Architec. & Arch. Soc. Durham & N'b'land*, x (1953), 374), but corroborative evidence is needed before the question can be considered settled.

[2] The often repeated statement that the legionary fortress at Chester was likewise involved in the disaster is now thought to be untrue, see I. A. Richmond and G. Webster, *Chester Arch. J.* XXXVIII (1951), 20–1; while, doubtless owing to its isolated situation, the auxiliary fort on the Lawe at South Shields also escaped unharmed.

Cassius Dio, whose *History*, in abridged form, constitutes the main literary source for this period, states that when Lupus arrived in Britain he found it overrun by a confederacy called the Maeatae; and that, unable to expel them by force, and to prevent them from concluding an alliance with their northern neighbours, the Caledonians, he was compelled to buy them off.[1] At a somewhat earlier date the Caledonians appear from Ptolemy's account of the Scottish tribes [2] to have been centred on the Great Glen, but by the end of the second century they too had given their name to a wider confederacy, which probably embraced not only Moray, but also Mar and Buchan—districts which Ptolemy assigns to the Vacomagi and Taexali. The Maeatae, on the other hand, are not mentioned by Ptolemy, and Dio, who describes them as a confederacy, does not locate them precisely, merely stating that they lived 'close to the Wall that cuts the island in two.' [3] Although Haverfield, Watson and others assumed that the wall in question was Hadrian's Wall, and on this basis sought to establish the Maeatae between the Forth and Tyne, it is now generally agreed that they dwelt, to the north of the Antonine Wall, in Strathearn, Strathmore and the Mearns.[4] Thus the Maeatae and the Caledonians between them dominated the whole of eastern Scotland from the Forth estuary at least as far north as the Moray Firth; and there can be little doubt that the chief reason for the Roman decision to reoccupy outpost forts in Strathearn, in Maeatian territory, when the frontier was advanced to the Forth-Clyde line under Antoninus Pius, had been to prevent a union between these powerful and hostile native groups. For the time being, Virius Lupus had no alternative but to use money to achieve the same end.

In a celebrated passage,[5] Dio gives what purports to be a description of the manners and customs of these peoples. Both tribes, he says, 'inhabit rugged hills with swamps between, possessing neither walled places nor towns nor

[1] Dio, LXXV, 5 [2] Ptolemy, *Geogr.* II, 3, 1–16 [3] Dio, LXXVI, 12
[4] F. T. Wainwright, *The Problem of the Picts* (1955), 51–2
[5] Dio, LXXVI, 12

cultivated lands, but living by pastoral pursuits and by hunting and on certain kinds of berries. They eat no fish, although their waters teem with all kinds of them. They live in tents, naked and shoeless; they have their women in common and rear all their offspring. Their government is democratic, and they take the utmost delight in forays for plunder. They fight from chariots, and have small, swift horses. Their infantry are extremely fleet of foot and enduring. Their weapons are a shield and a short spear with a knob of brass on the end of the butt . . . they have also daggers. They can endure hunger and thirst and every kind of hardship. They plunge into marshes, and last out many days with only their heads above water, and in the woods they live on bark and roots; and above all they prepare a certain food such that, if they eat only the bulk of a bean of it, they neither hunger nor thirst.' Unfortunately this account is such a strange compound of generalities and of travellers' tales that it is practically worthless, and archaeology has supplied little more substantial information to put in its place. That the Caledonian armament included war-chariots is confirmed by Tacitus' description of the battle of Mons Graupius,[1] and also by the recognition of a specifically Caledonian rein-ring, or terret, which was probably manufactured on Donside in the second or third century [2]; but otherwise the only distinctive native products from either region at this period are certain cast bronze spiral or penannular armlets decorated with enamel.[3] The assertion that the Maeatae and the Caledonians were a purely pastoral folk, living in tents, is, however, manifestly inaccurate, since a number of stone hut-clusters with earth-houses attached, which constitute the prevailing type of Iron-Age settlement in the regions in question, have produced evidence of occupation, and of cereal cultivation, in the second and third centuries; while, for

[1] Tac. *Agr.* 35, 3

[2] H. E. Kilbride-Jones, *PSAS* LXIX (1934–5), 448–53. Kilbride-Jones' arguments for an earlier date for this type of terret are not convincing.

[3] E. T. Leeds, *Celtic Ornament in the British Isles down to A.D.* 700 (1933), 126–30

what it is worth, two hills on the southern border of Maeatian territory, and which are linguistically connected with that tribe, namely Myot Hill and Dumyat, are both crowned by hill-forts.[1] Childe has suggested [2] that Dio's reference to the native practice of living in bogs may have been prompted by lake-dwellings (crannogs), numbers of which occur in the Highland lochs, but crannogs are equally common in south-west Scotland, and none of the Highland examples has yet furnished any definite proof of Iron-Age origin. Some of them, in fact, are known to have been inhabited as late as the sixteenth and seventeenth centuries. It might be thought that in general the account stems from descriptions of smaller and more particular tribal areas, erroneously applied to the whole.

South of the Forth-Clyde isthmus, the dispositions of the North British tribes are not thought to have undergone any material change throughout the second century. Thus, in the Lowlands, the Votadini continued to hold sway over Northumberland, Berwickshire and the Merse, while the Damnonii remained in possession of upper Clydesdale and Ayrshire. Between these two tribes, both of which appear to have been well-disposed towards Rome, Nithsdale and Galloway were presumably still occupied by the Novantae, and the middle and upper Tweed by the Selgovae. And to the south of Hadrian's Wall, the whole tract of territory as far as the Humber and Mersey, with the exception of the Yorkshire Wolds, was dominated by the Brigantes, who now possessed a Romanised capital at *Isurium* (Aldborough).

Building inscriptions show that Lupus began the task of repairing the defences immediately he reached Britain in 197. The work was evidently carried out systematically, the Yorkshire forts being the first to receive attention,[3] then those of Westmorland [4]; and by 208 a later Governor, Alfenus Senecio,

[1] F. T. Wainwright, loc. cit.

[2] V. G. Childe, *The Prehistory of Scotland* (1935), 257

[3] *CIL* VII, 210 (Ilkley), 273 (Bowes)

[4] *EE* VII, 951 (Brough-under-Stainmore)

had completed the restoration of Hadrian's Wall and of the outpost fort at Risingham in Northumberland.[1] Yet the mere reconstruction of the defences was not sufficient in itself to guarantee the immunity of the frontier from further attack, so long as the Caledonians and Maeatae remained unpunished. Both custom and the realities of the situation demanded that they should be taught a stern lesson. Accordingly preparations were made for a punitive campaign, and Severus, accompanied by his sons Caracalla and Geta, crossed to Britain to lead it in person. Owing to their hatred of Caracalla, who was the moving spirit behind the whole enterprise, both Dio[2] and his contemporary, Herodian,[3] write disparagingly of the subsequent operations, describing them as nothing more than guerilla warfare in which the Romans, vainly striving to bring the enemy to a pitched battle, and exposed to frequent ambushes, lost heavily in men and material. Nevertheless it is clear that at the time these campaigns were highly successful. The Caledonians, against whom the initial onslaught was directed, were reduced to unconditional surrender in the first season (209), and the Maeatae suffered a similar fate in the following year. The conditions imposed on the vanquished tribes, which included not only the surrender of territory but also the conscription of prisoners into the Roman army, were, however, so onerous as to produce a joint revolt in 210–11. At this moment, when preparing for a final campaign of extermination, Severus died at York, and Caracalla, so we are told, immediately broke off the action and came to terms with the barbarians, withdrawing his forces from their territory. On the other hand, the coin issues of the period indicate that the campaign envisaged by Severus was actually carried into effect, and, although both the Caledonians and the Maeatae survived it, its success may be gauged from the fact that thereafter, for nearly a hundred years, the northern frontier remained at peace.

[1] *CW*[2] XXX (1930), 199 (Birdoswald); *AA*[4] IX (1932), 233–4 (Housesteads); *AA*[4] XVI (1939), 240–2 (Chesters); *CIL* VII, 1003 (Risingham)

[2] Dio, LXXVI, 13

[3] Herodian, III, 8

Archaeology has so far shed scarcely any light on the Severan campaigns, but this is not surprising in view of their short duration and the fluid nature of the fighting. One depôt, where the stores required by the expeditions were stock-piled, has been identified at Corbridge,[1] and another, which is estimated to have been capable of holding sufficient grain to last 24,000 men for three months, at South Shields.[2] And from the latter port the supplies were evidently shipped to an advance base at Cramond, on the Forth, where an unusually high proportion of coins of Severus and his family have been found.[3] In view of Dio's statement that Severus, in his first campaign, reached ' almost to the extremity of the island,' it might be expected that some at least of the chain of marching-camps which extend in a great arc along the coastal plain from the South Esk to the Spey were built at this time, but proof is lacking; and, apart from Cramond, none of the permanent forts north of the outposts of Hadrian's Wall has produced any convincing evidence of occupation in the third century. It is true that Birley [4] and Miller [5] have argued, on somewhat different grounds, that the puzzling third period on the Antonine Wall, which Macdonald assigned to the years 184–5, really represents a re-occupation of the *limes* by Severus—either as a temporary measure to safeguard his rearward communications while campaigning farther north, or because he intended to re-establish, and perhaps to extend, the Antonine frontier system—but the coins and the pottery do not as yet furnish any support for this hypothesis.[6] Unfortunately we do not know what plans Severus had for consolidating the northern frontier, although the fact that no attempt was made to restore any forts north of the Cheviot

[1] E. Birley and I. A. Richmond, *AA*[4] xv (1938), 264
[2] I. A. Richmond, *AA*[4] xi (1934), 99
[3] G. Macdonald, *PSAS* lii (1917–18), 213–16
[4] E. Birley, *PSAS* lxxii (1937–8), 343–4
[5] S. N. Miller, *The Roman Occupation of SW Scotland* (1952), 235–9
[6] The scale of the third-period rebuilding at Cadder seems to forbid the assumption that only a temporary occupation was envisaged, see J. Clarke, *The Roman Fort at Cadder* (1933), 88–9.

before he set foot in Britain might seem to imply that it had already been decided to revert to the Tyne-Solway line as soon as the punitive campaigns had served their purpose. However this may be, the archaeological evidence leaves no room for doubt that when peace was finally concluded by Caracalla all Roman troops were evacuated from Scotland, apart from lower Annandale, and Hadrian's Wall once again became the fixed frontier. Nevertheless, as Richmond has convincingly demonstrated,[1] this strategic withdrawal was not simply a reversion to the Hadrianic system, but was accompanied by far-reaching changes in the organisation of the frontier defences. On the Wall itself the garrisons were substantially reinforced at vital points, the fort at Birdoswald, for example, now harbouring two cohorts, one of which was milliary. At the same time the dismantling of many of the turrets implies that the work of patrolling and signalling was drastically curtailed, while a similar relaxation of the precautions formerly taken to deal with local attacks is shown by the reduction in width of the milecastle gateways to mere foot-passages.[2] At first sight these changes appear inconsistent, yet they are easily reconciled in the light of the new arrangements in the forward area which now becomes the keystone of the whole frontier system.

Under Hadrian, outpost forts had been established in advance of the Wall, at Birrens, Netherby and Bewcastle, in order to give timely warning of the approach of raiding-parties, since the western sector of the Wall has only a limited outlook. Severus' lieutenants not only rebuilt these three forts,[3] but added two more to their number by reoccupying Risingham and High Rochester on Dere Street. The third-century arrangements at Birrens are still obscure, but the other four forts were equipped with stout defences and were strongly

[1] *Northumberland County History*, xv, 95–6

[2] J. C. Bruce, *Handbook to the Roman Wall* (10th edn., 1947), 26–8

[3] The case for a third-century occupation at Birrens, argued by E. Birley (see note 4, p. 96), has recently been strengthened by the discovery of a *denarius* of Severus Alexander within the defences of the second-century fort.

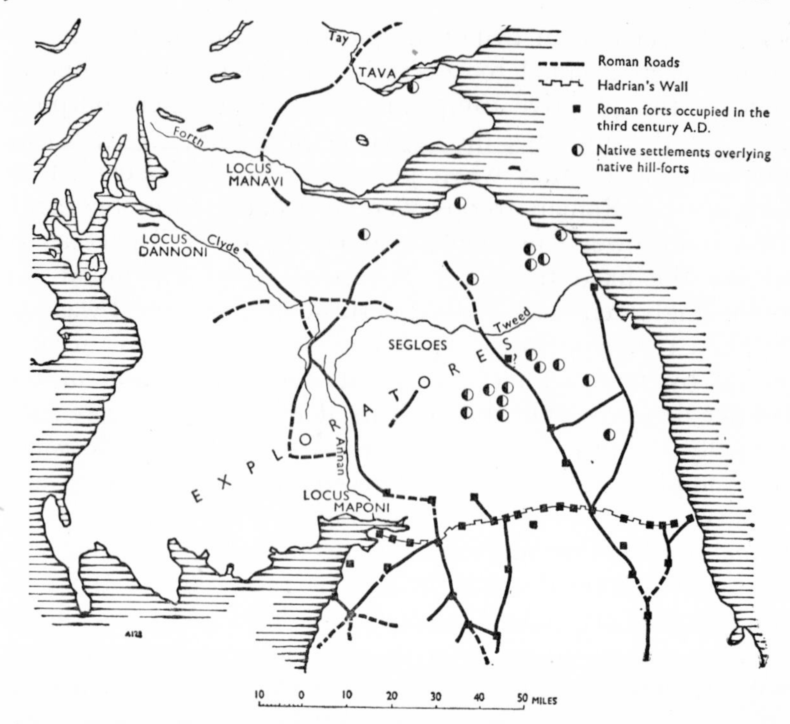

FIG. 2 The Northern Frontier in the Third Century A.D.

garrisoned. Each was given a part-mounted cohort, 1,000 strong, while Netherby, High Rochester and Risingham also served as the headquarters of irregular units known as *exploratores* or scouts.[1] Risingham even possessed a second unit of irregulars at this time—the *Raeti Gaesati*, or Tyrolese spearmen.[2] These *exploratores* represent an innovation on the British frontier, and since the forts on which they were based are too small to have housed them as well as the permanent garrisons, it follows that their function can only have been long-range patrolling; and this in turn pre-supposes the existence of scouting posts some distance in advance of the outpost forts. On the evidence of two Roman altars from Jedburgh Abbey, one of which was dedicated by the *Raeti*

[1] *Northumberland County History*, XV, 95–6 [2] *CIL* VII, 1002

Gaesati[1] and the other by a tribune of the 1st cohort of *Vardulli*,[2] the regular garrison at High Rochester in the third century, it seems probable that one such post lay in the vicinity of Jedburgh, if not at Jedburgh itself. And another may be represented by a Roman entrenchment, which has been recently discovered from the air near Tweedmouth, at the end of the Roman road from Corbridge to the Tweed, and has yielded a fragment of late third-century pottery.[3] On the east, therefore, there are some grounds for believing that the frontier patrols operated at least as far north as the Tweed, and it is reasonable to assume that the corresponding patrols in the central and western districts ranged equally far afield. In this manner the Wall defences were now reinforced by the creation of a deep zone of supervision and interception beyond them, and it is the added security afforded by this zone that explains the relaxation of precautions against local surprise attacks not only on the Wall, but also, it would seem, on the Cumberland coast.[4]

The Severan frontier system thus represents a marked advance on the systems which had preceded it. Hadrian's Wall, though effective enough as an obstacle, had not proved entirely satisfactory since it was out of touch with the main centres of resistance, while the shifting of the frontier to the Forth-Clyde isthmus under Antoninus Pius had imposed too great a strain on the limited manpower resources available to the Roman command. By re-establishing the continuous barrier on the Tyne-Solway line, and by turning the forward area into what was to all intents and purposes a protectorate, Caracalla and his successors not only dispensed with the need for a costly occupation of the Lowlands, but they ensured that, so long as the intelligence service provided by the *exploratores* functioned efficiently, the initiative would remain in Roman hands.

If, however, Roman literary and archaeological sources

[1] *EE*, VII, 1092 [2] G. Macdonald, *PSAS* LVII (1922–3), 173–7

[3] J. K. St. Joseph, *JRS* XLI (1951), 56

[4] F. G. Simpson and K. S. Hodgson, *CW*[2] XLVII (1947), 124

present a reasonably consistent picture of the Severan reorganisation, and of the events that led up to it, it must not be forgotten that this picture is one-sided and that the native sources have their own contribution to make. For it is obvious that the new policy would have little chance of success unless the Lowland tribes were prepared to co-operate with the frontier patrols, and analogies from other Roman frontiers suggest that the detailed arrangements—such as the precise limits of the patrolled zone, and the extent to which the tribesmen were allowed to build, or maintain, fortifications, and to administer their own day-to-day affairs—would be laid down by formal treaty. Logically, then, the next step in the inquiry is to see what information, if any, concerning the Severan reforms can be derived from the native sites themselves.

In south-western Scotland, and in the central Lowlands, the search is unrewarding, for very few of the forts and settlements in these regions have been examined, whether systematically or otherwise; and although several crannogs, caves and *duns* have yielded Roman potsherds and coins of late first- and second-century date,[1] only in one case has a third-century Roman relic been recovered from any of them. Clearly this negative evidence cannot be interpreted to mean that, as a result of the Severan reorganisation, this major portion of the forward zone became a prohibited area from which tribesmen were rigorously excluded. Nor can it imply that the Roman withdrawal to Hadrian's Wall severed all trade connections between the districts on either side of the Solway Firth, for Roman coins continued to circulate in the south-west and in the central Lowlands throughout the third century.[2] The most that can be said is that comparison of the coin finds suggests that trade was on a reduced scale compared with the second century, while the slender evidence provided by the excavated sites would appear to indicate that the evacuation of the Roman garrisons from their midst

[1] Cf. J. Curle, *PSAS* LXVI (1931–2), 367–83

[2] A. S. Robertson, *PSAS* LXXXIV (1949–50), 156

deprived the Selgovae, the Novantae and the Damnonii of the opportunities which they had previously enjoyed for acquiring small quantities of Roman pottery. But the competent investigation of only one or two native settlements in these areas may require even these modest conclusions to be drastically revised.

On the eastern flank of the forward zone, in the Tyne-Forth province, the situation is more encouraging, since considerable progress has been made within recent years in classifying the numerous Early-Iron-Age sites on both sides of the Border; and the general inferences which may be drawn from comprehensive field-surveys have been supplemented by excavation of several key-sites. In consequence of this work, and of the findings of previous investigators, it is now possible to distinguish three types of native sites which were occupied in the third century. First, in a class by itself, there is the hill-town (*oppidum*) of Traprain Law, in East Lothian, one of the principal towns, if not the capital, of the Votadini, which is known to have been inhabited almost continuously from Flavian times at least until the end of the fourth century.[1] The archaeological evidence conveys a hint of a temporary abandonment of the site at some period between the reigns of Antoninus Pius and Gallienus, and in view of the philo-Roman sympathies of the Votadini it would not be surprising if this abandonment was connected with the invasion of the Maeatae. But by the middle of the third century, if not before, the inhabitants of Traprain were once again receiving regular supplies of Roman goods; and these close trade relations carry with them the implication of equally close diplomatic relations which were doubtless maintained through regular meetings between Roman representatives and the tribal chieftains. We do not know, however, whether the town was fortified at this period, for although traces of three distinct defensive systems can still be seen on the hill, two

[1] For a recent appreciation of the Traprain excavations, and a bibliography, cf. A. H. A. Hogg in *Aspects of Archaeology in Britain and Beyond* (1951), 200–20

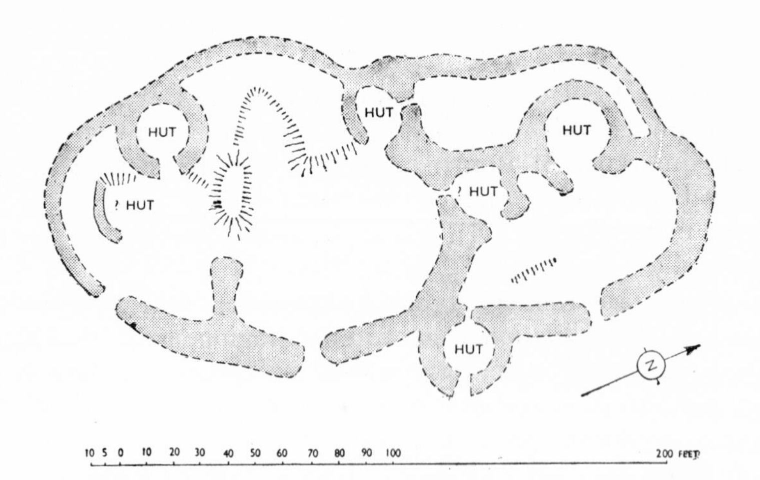

FIG. 3 Native Settlement, Cockburn Law, Berwickshire
(*Based on Crown copyright plans by permission of the Ancient Monuments* (*Scotland*) *Commission and the Controller of H.M. Stationery Office*)

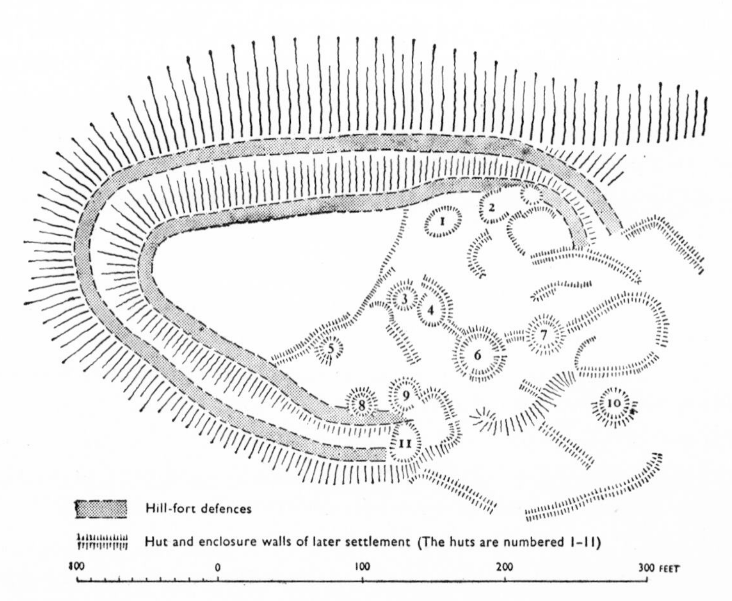

FIG. 4 Hill-fort and Settlement, Southdean Law, Roxburghshire
(*Based on Crown copyright plans by permission of the Ancient Monuments* (*Scotland*) *Commission and the Controller of H.M. Stationery Office*)

of these are not earlier than the late third or early fourth century, while the other is undated.[1]

The other two types of native sites which were occupied in the Tyne-Forth province in the third century are the stone-built settlements, or villages, and the stone-built homesteads. Both types are widely distributed throughout the region, but the main concentrations are to be found in the foothills on both sides of the Cheviots and around St Abb's Head. The settlements (Fig. 3) take the form of lightly protected, or unenclosed, clusters of from five to as many as forty round or oval stone huts, which rarely show any sign of deliberate planning except that they are sometimes grouped around scooped and walled courts. Such settlements are clearly a later development of the palisaded settlements containing wooden huts which were current in the locality until shortly before the Agricolan invasion,[2] and a date not earlier than the Roman period is similarly indicated by the fact that no less than nineteen of them overlie abandoned hill-forts,[3] including multivallate forts whose construction is now assigned to the late first century (Fig. 4). The earliest datable objects recovered from any of them belong, in fact, to the second century; but for our purposes it is sufficient to note that two typical examples of such settlements, Hownam Rings and Kaimes Hill, both of which sprawl over multivallate hill-forts, have produced third-century relics.[4] It can therefore be inferred that a fair proportion of them continued to function in the period following the Severan reorganisation.

Whereas the settlement evidently represents the establishment of a small community of farmers or herdsmen, the

[1] *Arch. News Letter* I, no. 5 (1948), 12

[2] E.g. Hayhope Knowe, C. M. Piggott, *PSAS* LXXXIII (1948–9), 45–67

[3] The sites in question are: Hownam Rings, Kirkton Hill, Morebattle Hill, Southdean Law, Park Law, Tamshiel Rig, Edgerston, Bonchester Hill and Mid Hill (Roxburghshire); Kaimes Hill (Midlothian); The Chesters, Drem (East Lothian); Cockburn Law, Coldingham Loch, Shannabank Hill, Marygold Hill Plantation, Edinshall and Longcroft (Berwickshire); Norman's Law (Fife); West Greaves Ash and Lordenshaws (Northumberland).

[4] C. M. Piggott, *PSAS* LXXXII (1947–8), 216–17; Macdonald, *PSAS* LII (1917–18), 235

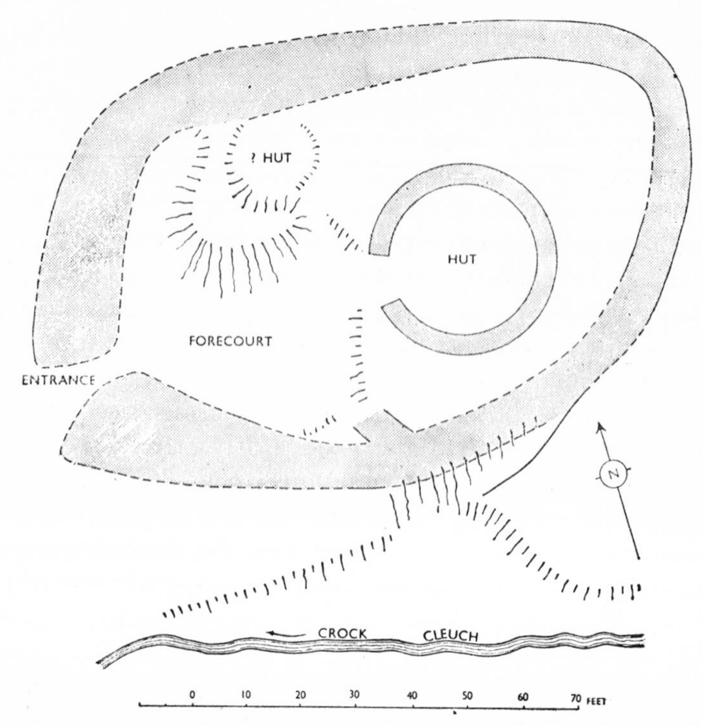

FIG. 5 East Homestead, Crock Cleuch, Roxburghshire

homestead was designed to house only a single family. Typical of this class are the two adjacent homesteads at Crock Cleuch, Roxburghshire,[1] each of which consisted of a large, round stone hut standing within an oval walled compound (Fig. 5), though rectilinear compounds are found at Hownam Rings, Kidlaw [2] and elsewhere. As in the case of the settlements, the stone-built homesteads are doubtless derived from timber prototypes, such as the palisaded structures on Gray Coat and Greenbrough Hill,[3] and do not seem to have appeared in the Tyne-Forth province before the Roman period, although there is both literary and archaeological evidence for their survival into the Dark Ages. Thus the homesteads at Hownam

[1] K. A. Steer and G. S. Keeney, *PSAS* LXXXI (1946–7), 138–57
[2] RCAM *East Lothian*, no. 259
[3] C. M. Piggott, *PSAS* LXXXIII (1948–9), 65–7

Rings, South Berryfell,[1] Kidlaw, Green Craig,[2] and an unpublished example on Glenduckie Hill (Fife), are all later than hill-forts, while excavation has shown that the Crock Cleuch sites were occupied from about the second to the sixth or seventh century. And it has been observed that the description of the hermitage which St Cuthbert erected on Farne Island suggests that it was modelled on structures of this class, which must, therefore, have been current during the saint's lifetime.[3]

How many of these homesteads and settlements were in existence in the third century, and how many are of earlier or later date will, of course, never be known; nor can a comprehensive distribution-map of the surviving examples, irrespective of date, be prepared until Hogg's admirable work in classifying the native sites in Northumberland [4] has been followed up by detailed field surveys of the individual monuments. Nevertheless, it can safely be said that, so far as the Lowlands are concerned, the geographical limits of both groups closely conform to those of the settlements overlying hill-forts. When these are plotted (Fig. 2) it is seen that, apart from one outlier (Norman's Law) in Fife, they all fall within, or on the fringe of, Votadinian territory. The published *Reports* of the Scottish Ancient Monuments Commission and the results of recent unpublished field work by that body, make it clear that settlements and homesteads of the types under discussion are virtually non-existent in the Tweed basin, the heart of the Selgovian country, and in the territories of the Novantae and Damnonii. Yet to the south of Hadrian's Wall both types occur freely in Westmorland, and, indeed, form one of the most striking features of the archaeology of that county.[5]

[1] RCAM *Roxburghshire*, I (1956), 109
[2] G. Bersu, *PSAS* LXXXII (1947–8), 272–3
[3] I. A. Richmond, *Antiquity* XV (1941), 88–9
[4] A. H. A. Hogg, *Antiquity* XVII (1943), 136–47 and *PSAN*[4] XI (1946–1950), 140–79
[5] RCHM *Westmorland, passim.* It has been observed that the complicated appearance of some of the Westmorland 'villages,' such as Ewe Close (p. 84),

The evidence from the native sites on the eastern flank of the forward zone would seem therefore to suggest the following conclusions :

(i) The Severan reorganisation led to no perceptible change in the *modus vivendi* of the rank and file of the tribesmen, who continued to dwell as peacefully in their villages or crofts as did their fellow-countrymen sheltered behind the barrier of Hadrian's Wall.

(ii) Except perhaps in special cases, such as Traprain Law, native fortifications were prohibited, while, in return, law and order were guaranteed by the Roman command operating through the *exploratores*.

(iii) Trade between Roman and Native continued throughout the third century, but was mainly focused on Traprain Law. This is no doubt due, in part, to the fact that Traprain, as a manufacturing town, had more to offer the Roman market than the rural settlements whose economy was barely raised above subsistence level, but it probably also reflects the growing importance of the place as an administrative centre in close liaison with Rome.

(iv) If the native settlement on Norman's Law is third century—and this has yet to be decided—the district watched over by the *exploratores* must have extended to the Tay. Thus the transference of the Stirlingshire plain from the Maeatae to the Votadini, which was an accomplished fact by the end of the fourth century, may well have been foreshadowed by the Severan reorganisation. Dio, indeed, states that the Maeatae were compelled to cede no small amount of territory.

Otherwise the regulations which governed the establishment of the Lowland protectorate were no doubt similar to those imposed on certain native tribes beyond the Danube,

---

is the result either of a later expansion, or of successive reconstructions, of an original nucleus, so that these cannot be strictly compared with the larger Votadinian settlements, like that on Kaimes Hill, where the surviving huts all appear to represent a single occupation. On the other hand, the smaller Westmorland settlements (e.g. Kentmere p. 131), and the homesteads (e.g. Bampton Towtop Kirk p. 33), find exact counterparts in the Cheviot foothills.

where Roman protectorates were set up in the latter half of the second century.[1] There the boundaries of the tribes were formally defined; the amount of tribute to be paid, whether in grain or in recruits for the Roman army, was laid down; and tribal assemblies for trade and other purposes were strictly limited to fixed times and places under Roman supervision. One of the first requirements of a primitive frontier organisation is the appointment of trysting-places where justice can be administered and markets held, and Professor Richmond has pointed out [2] that there is one Roman source which seems to indicate the existence of an arrangement of this kind on the northern frontier of Britain. For in the British section of the Ravenna Cosmography, a list of geographical names which was compiled from various sources, and principally from Roman road-books, in the seventh century, there occurs a list of seven *loca*, or meeting-places—*Maponi*, *Mixa*, *Panovius*, *Minox*, *Taba*, *Manavi*, *Segloes* and *Dannoni*. Three of these places (*Mixa*, *Panovius* and *Minox*) cannot now be identified, but *Taba* is evidently a scribal error for *Tava*, the Tay, while *Segloes* and *Dannoni* presumably lay respectively within the territories of the Selgovae and the Damnonii. In the two remaining cases more precise identifications are possible, for there are good etymological grounds for connecting *Maponi* with the Clochmabenstane, a large boulder which once formed part of a megalithic monument on the Solway shore, south of Gretna, and which was a recognised place of assembly in early mediaeval times. And similarly, since well-known megalithic monuments would obviously provide convenient focal points for tribal gatherings, it is tempting to suggest that *Manavi*, which is linked with *Manau*, the district at the head of the Firth of Forth, was located in the vicinity of the *Clack Mannan*, or stone of *Manau*,[3] which originally stood not far from its present position in the centre of Clackmannan town. If it were certain that this list reflects the Severan

[1] Dio, LXXI, 15–16, 19; LXXII, 2–3
[2] *Northumberland County History*, XV, 97
[3] RCAM *Fife*, no. 612

arrangements, the inclusion of *Tava* and *Manavi* would provide the necessary proof for the suggestion advanced above that Roman control in the third century extended as far north as the Tay; but although such meeting-places are more likely to have been established in a protectorate than in an occupied zone, an Antonine date cannot be entirely ruled out since a number of forts on the Antonine Wall are named in the section of the Cosmography to which the list of *loca* is appended.

Up to this point we have been considering the Severan reorganisation as a calculated piece of military strategy designed for the sole purpose of stabilising the northern frontier. Yet the outstanding feature of this frontier in the third century is not merely that it remained at peace, but that relations between the Roman garrison and the natives dwelling in the districts adjacent to the Wall continued to improve. Many local native deities, for instance, which had previously been driven underground, now emerged from obscurity and found worshippers from amongst the troops stationed on, or close to, the Wall. To some extent this increased accord was no doubt due to the consciousness of unity created by Roman rule, and to the growing menace from the barbarians beyond the Tay and across the Irish Sea. But the most important factor which stimulated a more friendly atmosphere was unquestionably the change in the composition of the frontier garrison. From the time of Augustus onwards regiments stationed on the frontiers of the empire were often brought up to strength by enlisting recruits from amongst the local tribesmen, but this practice does not seem to have been adopted to any extent in Britain in the first and second centuries—presumably because the province was too restless to allow the employment of British auxiliaries on its frontiers. From the third century, however, local recruiting for the auxiliaries became standard practice in Britain as elsewhere, and although the individual regiments still retained their old territorial names, these names no longer had any significance so far as the composition of the units was concerned. Nor is there any reason to suppose that these recruits were necessarily the reluctant victims of the Roman press-gangs, for obviously a frontier force of this kind could only function successfully so long as the rank and file willingly identified themselves with the cause of imperial defence. Indeed, at a time when tribal enmity was still stronger than national feeling, a career in the Roman army must have offered considerable attractions to native warriors whose traditional means of livelihood—by pillaging their neighbours' goods—had been suppressed by the *pax Romana*. Thus, early in the third century, we find a unit of ' British Volunteers,' possibly from the Scottish Lowlands or even from farther north, stationed at Walldürn, on the German frontier.[1] And it has been suggested that the Caledonian chieftain, Lossio Veda, who dedicated an altar at Colchester in the reign of Severus Alexander (222–35), was posted there in some official capacity connected with the movement of recruits from North Britain to the middle Rhine.[2] The natural consequence of local recruiting was, of course, that the army gradually lost its alien character and assumed the aspect of a national militia ; and this process was further stimulated by an edict of Severus which permitted soldiers to marry while on active service, and also by a decree of Severus Alexander allowing frontier troops to lease land on condition that their sons were serving in the army. As a result the small civil settlements housing camp-followers and traders, which had probably always existed outside the walls of the forts in the hinterland of the occupied territory, underwent considerable expansion ; and henceforward such settlements regularly appear in association with the forts directly in the front line. In the third and fourth centuries all the forts on Hadrian's Wall, and the outpost forts beyond, possessed extensive extramural settlements, or *vici*. These accommodated not only the wives and families of the soldiers, but also retired veterans, itinerant traders and official travellers, and their official status was recognised in some cases by the

[1] H. T. Rowell, *Yale Classical Studies*, VI (1939), 102–3
[2] I. A. Richmond, *Arch. J.* CIII (1946), 64

conferment of a degree of self-government. Although the transformation of these forts into miniature garrison towns, manned by 'territorials,' was a gradual process, and did not reach its maximum development until the fourth century, the stability which the northern frontier enjoyed in the third century is in no small measure attributable to the influence of the *vici*. For by giving the garrisons a stake in the land they diminished the risk of revolt: and at the same time they furnished a strong link between the native population and the official military régime.

In spite of this more cordial atmosphere, however, it is clear that Romanisation made no great headway amongst the bulk of the tribesmen dwelling on the northern frontier in the third century. Of the native sites we have been discussing, only Traprain has afforded the slightest grounds for suspicion that Romanising influences were consciously at work, and for the rest the native shepherds and cultivators were seemingly left in peace apart from the periodical attentions of the tax-collector and the recruiting sergeant. And they, for their part, were evidently content to carry on in their old ways, living in homesteads and settlements of traditional pattern, and acquiring little or nothing from Roman sources except for occasional coins and potsherds. This state of affairs is not peculiar to the Votadini and the rest of the Lowland tribes, but is equally applicable to the Romano-British peasant-farmers in Westmorland, West Yorkshire, Wales, and even on the Downs of southern England.

To sum up, the Severan reorganisation represents a transitional stage in the history of the northern frontier in Roman times. For whereas the previous systems had been based almost entirely on force, the Severan system, while retaining the ultimate authority in Roman hands, invited the Lowland tribes to become partners in the common cause of preserving peace. And we have seen that acceptance of this invitation was made easier by the fact that, throughout the third century, the army of occupation was losing its alien character and taking root in the soil. Thus the way was prepared for the even more remarkable development in the following century, when responsibility for the defence of the northern frontier was transferred from the Roman army to the federate native kingdoms of the Damnonii and the Votadini.

Chapter V

ROMAN AND NATIVE IN THE FOURTH CENTURY A.D., AND AFTER

ON the northern frontier of Britain the fourth century opened with a situation which fairly closely repeated the disastrous events of A.D. 197. The Wall garrison had been withdrawn [1] in 296 to fight for the usurper-Emperor Allectus against the central government, and the fact that his defeat by Constantius Caesar took place in southern Britain instead of southern Gaul did not prevent the northern tribes from seizing the moment of confused transition to invade and plunder the province. On this occasion also the damage went deep [2]: a century before the legionary fortress at York had fallen, but this time Chester was also taken and had to be largely rebuilt, together with the forts of northern England, the Wall and its outposts. The Roman reaction, however, was more vigorous and rapid, no doubt because this time the Wall garrison, and perhaps the legions too, returned intact to their stations [3] and could be set to fight and rebuild more rapidly than under Severus, when a largely new army of Britain had been needed.[4] The Wall and its outposts were rebuilt by A.D. 305, as the Birdoswald inscription [5] shows, while Constantius, now become

[1] This is a fair inference from the fact that Allectus did not deploy all his forces (*Pan.* v, 16: nec omnes copias quas trahebat instruxerit), and from the fact that although the forts were destroyed their third-century garrisons returned. The men cannot therefore have perished with their forts and must have been elsewhere.

[2] York: R. E. M. Wheeler, *JRS* XVI (1926), 193; Chester: Richmond and Webster, *Chester Arch. J.* XXXVIII (1950), 20–1

[3] The close, but not complete, correspondence between the third-century garrisons and the list of Wall forts in the *Notitia Dignitatum* proves this: see E. Birley, *CW*[2] XXXIX (1939), 199

[4] See E. Birley, *Beiträge zur älteren Europäischen Kulturgeschichte: Festschrift für Rudolf Egger* (1952–3), I,184–5

[5] *JRS* XIX (1929), 214–15

Emperor, spent the last year of his life in a campaign, described only in the most general terms in contemporary panegyrics,[1] but plainly involving the distant North and Pictish territory. The Severan pattern of operations was thus repeated. First came the campaigning to make the Wall area safe, then the rebuilding of the Wall and its forts, and, finally, the punitive action which imposed Roman terms upon the Picts and settled frontier affairs for the future. But while under Severus the first action did not start until A.D. 205, eight years after the recovery of the province, under Constantius the corresponding year saw the sequence of events coming to a close; so much quicker had been the Roman retaliation.

Any notion that Roman power and energy was on the wane will be dispelled by a glance at the masonry [2] of the period upon such sites as High Rochester, Corbridge or Chesterholm. These were, indeed, the restoration of older forts and their planning is often conservative and in truth old-fashioned. But work of the new age is seen in the multangular tower [3] and adjacent curtain-wall at York. There is also discernible the new style in tactics, even in the North. On the Saxon shore the great forts [4] built under Constantius and the usurper-Emperors whose dominion he recovered were almost all in the new manner, with projecting bastions and immensely high and strong curtain-walls. At Lancaster [5] a Constantian fort of the same kind has been detected. But in the open country-side, away from the coastline, new dispositions of troops are seen. The very large forts [6] at Piercebridge and Elslack, the

[1] *Pan.* VII, 7: cuius etiam suprema illa expeditio non Britannica trophaea, ut vulgo creditum est, expetivit, sed dis iam vocantibus ad intimum terrarum limen accessit . . . ut fruiturus exinde luce perpetua iam viderit illic diem paene continuum.

[2] High Rochester, *Northumberland County History*, XV, 88, plate; Corbridge, *AA*[4] XXVIII (1950), pl. XII; Chesterholm, *AA*[4] XIII (1936), pl. XVIII, 2

[3] S. N. Miller, *JRS* XVIII (1928), 78–82, fig. 21

[4] Collingwood, *Archaeology of Roman Britain* (1930), 50, fig. 11; 52, fig. 12

[5] *Hist. Soc. Lancs. & Cheshire*, CV (1953), 8–10

[6] Piercebridge, G. S. Keeney, *Trans. Architec. & Arch. Soc. Durham & N'b'land*, IX pt. i (1939), 45, fig. 1; Elslack: T. May, *YAJ* XXI (1910–11), 113–67

latter furnished with new-style gateways, represent a concentration of mobile striking forces at points of great tactical significance. Elslack guards the Aire Gap, preventing penetration by raiders landing in the Ribble or Morecambe Bay: Piercebridge blocks middle Teesdale, and protects the northern end of the Vale of York. Newton Kyme,[1] shielding lower Airedale and Calderdale, might well be another member of the same series. These arrangements have at first sight little to do with the northern frontier. When, however, it is appreciated that their function was to prevent the disorganisation of its rearward economy by sea-raiders, and at the same time to counter deep thrusts, the relevance of the matter becomes clear, and it becomes evident also that the new government had a plan for Northern Britain which reflected current practice in the military field.

As has already been observed, the troops returned to the frontier itself after their withdrawal by Allectus, virtually unchanged. This conclusion, however, applies to the old-standing regiments whose names are quoted[2] by the *Notitia Dignitatum*, in the section *per lineam valli*. The irregular forces which had been stationed with them, in such forts as Housesteads, are not mentioned again, except when, as with the *numerus Maurorum Aballavensium*[3] at Aballava (Burgh-by-Sands) the irregulars seem to have taken full charge and perhaps to have been upgraded. The *Notitia* has nothing whatever to say of the outpost forts, which, as is described below, were not given up until later in the century, and, failing inscriptions up to date, the fourth-century garrisons of these remain unknown. The folk based upon them, however, originally known as the *exploratores*, are now called, in the text[4] of Ammianus Marcellinus, *areani*. This is usually emended to *arcani*, or secret

[1] St. Joseph, *JRS* XLIII (1953), 87, pl. XI, 1

[2] *Not. Dign., Occ.* XL, 33–49

[3] ibid. 47: for a full commentary on this regiment, see E. Birley, *CW*[2] XXXIX (1939), 192–4.

[4] XXVIII, 3, 8; areanos genus hominum a veteribus institutum. For the connection of *areani* with *areae*, see C. E. Stevens, *Latomus* XIV (1955), 395

agents; yet Ammianus describes [1] their work as open frontier patrolling, in terms which might just as well have been used of the *exploratores*. But the *exploratores* had been out-stationed,[2] there being no room for them in the tightly packed garrison forts. If, then, they now lived in homesteads, these structures, so typical of the frontier region, might most appropriately have been described as *areae*, or sheep-folds, for that is precisely what many of them were: and such a settlement as Tamshiel Rig,[3] exceptionally large and solid, might represent their family house, when they were not specifically on duty. A close contact with the commercial needs of the area is made upon Hadrian's Wall at Housesteads, where at the beginning of the fourth century a special gateway [4] was built at Knag Burn to take civilian traffic through the Wall itself. Its design is of particular significance for regulations. Doors are provided both at the front and the rear of the single gateway passage, which was controlled from two guard-chambers and could be opened and closed like a canal lock, while a limited number of travellers was searched or taxed or otherwise supervised. Traders on their way northwards could thus be examined for contraband. Folk from the North could pass through into the Roman province proper, and many no doubt came in order to buy and sell in the market-village or *vicus* [5] which had grown up under the shelter of the Wall outside the fort at Housesteads. The *vicus* at this period was a large one, covering about 10 acres, and its buildings were in some degree planned: for example, outside the south gate of the fort they were strictly aligned [6] upon the road leading up to the west portal of the gate, the east portal having now been blocked in conformity with contemporary fashion. Air

[1] ibid.; id enim illis erat officium, ut ultro citroque per longa spatia discurrentes vicinarum gentium strepitus nostris ducibus intimarent.

[2] *Northumberland County History*, XV, 95–6

[3] RCAM, *Roxburghshire*, II, 426-7, figs. 565, 566,

[4] Birley, *AA*[4] XIV (1937), 172–7, fig. 1 and pl. XXIV for an account of the gate

[5] Birley and Charlton, *AA*[4] IX (1932), 232; cf. Richmond, *JRS* XXII (1932), 236

[6] Birley and Charlton, *AA*[4] X (1933), 90; cf. *AA*[4] XII (1935), pl. XXII

photography [1] shows the settlement extending widely, and there can be no doubt that it owed its size not merely to commerce with the garrison and with folk behind the Wall, but with the land of the *areani* beyond it. Its houses were on the whole remarkably uniform, and their commercial character is strongly reflected in their plan. Most of them have an open front about 15 feet wide, usually subdivided by a central pier, which carried the beam bearing the front of an upper storey: it also subdivided the front below it into bays suitable for movable shutters which were set in a groove like those of a market stall. Much of the lower floor is normally an open space, large enough to use as a shop or tavern, and only the back is subdivided into small rooms for service, whether cooking, storage or accounting. Many such shops and taverns still exist in our smaller towns. The upper storey would accordingly accommodate the family, and may, as in reliefs [2] which show such houses, have been furnished with a balcony. Here was room for variety of treatment which would break the monotony of planning, just as the colour-washes, with which the masonry and half-timber work was covered, or the shop signs and inn signs would catch and divert the eyes of the public. This much must be said in order to clothe the ground-plan with lively reality. It emphasises also an important difference between the living standards and economic possibilities of native villages, on either side of the Wall, and those of the Romanised *vicus*, where life was nearer burgher level. In the early fourth century this was the outstanding contrast between the land behind the Wall and the land beyond it. Fell homesteads [3] in Westmorland or North Yorkshire would have been difficult to distinguish from those of Roxburghshire [4]: both are the closely identical products of native life at shepherd or peasant level. But to the north of the Wall it

[1] St Joseph, *JRS* XLI (1951), pl. V

[2] A. Grenier, in Déchelette's *Manuel d'archéologie préhistorique celtique et gallo-romaine*, VI, pt. 2, 202, fig. 68; cf. Cichorius, *Die Reliefs der Traianssaüle*, sc. III, LXXXVI, LXXXIX, the last only with balcony

[3] p. 106 above, footnote

[4] See RCAM, *Roxburghshire* (1956), I, 19-21, for types

is not known for certain that any *vici* were now inhabited,[1] and it is sure that north of the Cheviot all were obliterated. But south of the Wall every important or old-established fort was surrounded by a large *vicus*,[2] obviously forming the commercial centre or market-villages of the district to which it belonged. Most of these centres were sprawling and large, with plans which were much influenced by ribbon development. They do not appear to have been walled, and the walled township, which represents a higher and more extensive grade of urban development, is normally the site which troops have left and where civilian life has taken root upon its own, as at Catterick (*Caturactonium*) or Carlisle (*Luguvalium*), and usually exceeds the ordinary *vicus* in size. For example, Catterick [3] is reckoned at 18 acres, Carlisle [4] at above 74, if it was indeed so large, while Corbridge covers some 40 acres, so far as its limits are known. The normal *vicus* outside a fort will rarely exceed 12 acres, and is often not nearly so big. But, large or small, the places must have exercised a considerable influence upon their environment and represent in themselves a nucleus of settlement to Romanised pattern which had no counterpart in the outlands. Their number and ubiquity should be emphasised. In Northumberland substantial fourth-century *vici* are known outside the forts of Wallsend, Rudchester, Halton, Chesters, Carrawburgh, Housesteads and Chesterholm; in Co. Durham, South Shields, Ebchester, Lanchester, Chester-le-Street, Binchester and Piercebridge; in Cumberland, Stanwix, Bowness, Old Carlisle, Maryport, Ravenglass, Old Penrith and Papcastle; in Westmorland, Brougham, Kirby Thore, Brough-under-Stainmore, Ambleside and Watercrook; in Lancashire, Overborough, Lancaster, Ribchester, Manchester; in Yorkshire, Newton Kyme, Malton, Brough-by-Bainbridge, Greta

[1] It is significant that the fourth-century repairs to the wall of Risingham were effected with civilian tombstones, see *Northumberland County History*, XV, 139–40; they are *CIL* VII, 1011, 1014, 1015 and 1019.

[2] For a list of such *vici*, see below, on this page.

[3] Hildyarde and Wade, *YAJ* XXXVII (1948–51), 522, figs. 1, 2

[4] Shaw, *CW*[2] XXIV (1924), 95

Bridge and Ilkley. The thirty-four here enumerated are more numerous than all the cities of Britain catalogued by Gildas,[1] and do not include a single one of them.

As has already been remarked, the commercial substitute for the *vicus* in the outlands was the periodic fair [2] or market, and of these too little is known. Economically, however, they represent a slower and lower rate of trade. But their existence is amply attested, in eastern Scotland at least, by the material from Traprain Law, and it need not be supposed that Traprain was the only *oppidum* of its kind in the Votadinian territory concerned. The material itself includes a good deal of money,[3] indicating that trade was not confined to barter, as, for example, among the Britons of Lundy Island [4] under Roman rule. The objects bought were mostly iron tools, but also the durable coarse pottery, which the native kilns could not produce, and some glass, no doubt reserved for better use. They indicated a low if steady expenditure upon necessities, with little luxury: and it must be remembered that all the perishable articles of wood, leather or horn, and all the textiles or furs have vanished from the scene and render the picture so much the more bare. But if these tribesfolk, a motley lot, or their chiefs, were compared with the burghers [5] of Carlisle, as they appear on their tombstones, it would become clear that the difference is between shepherd or peasant culture and urbanity, without that intermixture between the two which the Roman world continually produced. It is interesting that in such surroundings as Traprain Law anyone should have

[1] Gildas, *De Excidio*, 3: see the brilliant commentary on this by C. E. Stevens, *EHR* LII (1937), 193 ff.

[2] On fairs and markets near the frontier, see Birley and Keeney, *AA*[4] XII (1935), 218–23.

[3] The coins are enumerated by Sir George Macdonald, *PSAS* LVIII (1923–4), 326–7, the fourth-century list being impressive.

[4] Solinus, *Coll. Rer. Mem.* (Ed. Mommsen), 22, 7: Siluram quoque insulam ab ora quam gens Britanna Dumnonii tenent turbidum fretum distinguit. Cuius homines etiam nunc custodiunt morem vetustum; nummum refutant; dant res et accipiunt, mutationibus necessaria potius quam pretiis parant.

[5] *Catalogue of the Roman inscribed & sculptured stones in Carlisle Museum, Tullie House* (2nd ed., 1922), 37, no. 103, 38, no. 105

been troubling to learn the Roman alphabet. Yet it was so,[1] and this reflects a side of intercourse with the Roman province which is again little understood, representing the need to read Roman inscriptions and perhaps even Roman documents, the kind of accomplishment most necessary among merchants or chiefs. This interest in primary things does not, however, reflect culture or its acquisition: it is another aspect of everyday needs comparatively modest in scale, related to a background of tough daily life.

In the earlier fourth century the policies observable in the later third century are thus continued, and with success. As then, our evidence for relationship of Native and Roman comes from the east, and nothing satisfactory is known of the state of affairs in the west. It is not in the least likely that disorder was chronic. But in A.D. 343 there was a crisis, sufficiently alarming to bring the Emperor Constans [2] across the Channel in mid-winter. The fate which has deprived the historian of Roman Britain of some important chapters of Tacitus has befallen also a vital passage of Ammianus Marcellinus, in which he recounted [3] the *acta Constantis*. But his surviving cross-reference to the lost passage is linked with the *areani*, and this fact indicates both that the trouble was on the northern frontier of Britain, and that the *areani* were somehow involved. Further, archaeological evidence indicates [4] that about now the forts in the zone beyond the Wall were destroyed, and that in the restoration which followed High Rochester was left derelict while Risingham and Bewcastle were retained. The fate of Netherby remains unknown; even its early fourth-century occupation [5] is only to be divined from

[1] J. Curle, *PSAS* LXVI (1931–2), 359, fig. 42, showing two examples, including an alphabet

[2] *Cod. Theod.* XI, 74, 1 for a January edict at Boulogne: Firmicus, *De Error. Profan. Relig.* 28, 6. mutato ac contempto temporum ordine, hieme, quod nec factum est aliquando nec fiet, tumentes ac saevientibus undas calcastis Oceani. Sub remis vestris incogniti iam nobis paene maris unda contremuit, et insperatam imperatoris faciem Britannus expavit.

[3] XXVIII, 3, 8 areanos . . . super quibus aliqua in actibus Constantis retulimus.

[4] *Northumberland County History*, XV, 114

[5] Birley, *CW*² LIII (1953), 6–39

the fact that so many third-century inscriptions were re-used in a later restoration of the fort. Given, however, the peaceful relations with the East, the moves look like retrenchment there and continued concentration in the West. The reason which dictated retention of Risingham was no doubt the value of the iron-ore deposits there conveniently available to the military forges [1] for tools and weapons at Corbridge. It should, however, be emphasised that a disturbance sufficiently serious to demand the Emperor's presence is not likely to have been confined solely to the zone beyond the Wall, and that nervousness in urban areas is indicated also by the drastic reorganisation of the fortifications at places as far apart as Caerwent [2] and Great Casterton.[3] It might be suspected that raids from the Irish Sea were beginning to upset the peace not only of the northern outlands but the British provinces as well. Ammianus provides [4] an echo of still more trouble in the sixties, when 'places near the frontier were devastated.' The word used is *loca*, and it will be recalled that this is the word employed [5] for places of assembly for markets and the like among the frontier tribes. Again, the early recollections of St Jerome, which must belong to about this period, include Atecotti invading Gaul and allegations [6] of their taste for succulent portions of human flesh. Whatever the homeland of the Atecotti,[7] it is clear that they belonged either to Ireland

[1] *Northumberland County History*, XV, 80: Birley and Richmond, *AA*[4] XVII (1940), 113–14

[2] MOW Guide, *Caerwent Roman City, Monmouthshire* (1951), 7

[3] Corder, *Arch. J.* CXII (1955), 32–6

[4] A.D. 365, XXVI, 4, 5. Picti Saxonesque et Scotti et Atacotti Britannos aerumnis vexavere continuis: A.D. 360, XX, 1, 1 in Britanniis cum Scotorum Pictorumque gentium ferarum excursus, rupta quiete condicta, loca limitibus vicina vastarunt.

[5] Birley and Richmond, *Archaeologia* XCIII (1949), 15; cf. Dio LXXI, 15; LXXII, 2

[6] Jerome, *adv. Iovinianum*, II, 335 (ed., Migne, vol. 23), referring to years before A.D. 375; ipse adulescentulus in Gallia viderim Atticotos, gentem Brittannicam, humanis vesci carnibus . . . pastorum nates et feminarum (et) palpillas solere abscindere et has solas ciborum delicias arbitrari.

[7] See Ridgway, *JRS* XIV (1924), 135

or to the west coast of Scotland, and that by the middle of the century in the western seas their raiding was becoming a serious menace. It was doubtless to take stock of the early development of the situation and to concert effective counter-measures that Constans crossed the Channel in January: the intention cannot have been to undertake campaigning either by sea or land, though it may well have been the response to severe raiding in the quiet autumn weather.

In A.D. 367–9 the raiding took an especially severe turn, for which Ammianus is once more the authority. There was, he indicates,[1] a *barbarica conspiratio*, that is, 'a secret plan for concerted action among the barbarians,' by which all those interested in plundering the British province were to attack it at once. Accordingly, Franks, Saxons, Atecotti and Scoti invaded[2] at once, pinned down Nectaridus, Duke of the British province, who should have been on the move with the field army, and killed the Count of the Saxon Shore, whose name *Fullofaudes* or *Bulchobaudes* is German, like the contemporary general Merobaudes. The events indeed seemed like the result of a *conspiratio*, and it will be recalled that the Roman Empire had its interpreters[3] attached to the forces for dealing with prisoners and that interrogation may have elicited specific evidence for such action. However this may be, the results in economic loss and damage were serious enough. Archaeologically, it is not easy to assess in the civilian areas: but in the North the traces are written large on the Wall at least. The damage was very serious. All the forts and all the civilian settlements outside them had been sacked and burnt and stood in need of rebuilding. In the rearward zone similar damage has been detected[4] at Cor-

[1] XXXVII, 8, 1. Britannias indicabat barbarica conspiratione ad ultimam vexatas inopiam.

[2] ibid. Nectaridumque comitem maritimi tractus occisum et Fullofaudem ducem hostium insidiis circumventus: for the invaders, see XXVII, 8, 5. The *comes maritimi tractus* is a literary version of the 'Count of the Saxon Shore.'

[3] von Domaszewski, *Rangordnung des röm. Heeres* (Bonn 1908), 37

[4] Birley and Richmond, *AA*[4] xv (1938), 262 (Corbridge); Keeney, *Trans. Architec. & Arch. Soc. Durham & N'b'land,* x pt. iii (1950), 308 (Piercebridge)

bridge, Piercebridge and Malton on the east, and at Overborough in the west. The legionary fortresses were not affected, for this time their garrisons were not absent. There were occasional escapes; for example, no contemporary destruction is apparent in the fort at South Shields,[1] though it was certainly involved in the military reorganisation which followed. Before rebuilding took place, however, there were grave faults in discipline to be corrected. According to Ammianus, Count Theodosius, who was in charge of the task, found that there were too many deserters.[2] This would imply that soldiers fled from their posts and faded into the civilian populace, an action easier to understand after well over a century of recruiting of units within the province and of land tenure based upon hereditary army service. An amnesty and pardon restored [3] many of them to the army. The *areani*, on the other hand, were abolished. They had treasonably made common cause with the enemy,[4] who had bribed them by promises of a share in the booty. This, too, is easy to comprehend, though not to pardon. The *areani* were outstationed and in daily contact with the outland tribes: and their geographical distribution, now overwhelmingly western, linked them with the traditionally, unreliable area where whatever its ostensible political state, dislike of Rome was plainly a tradition. The consequences had been serious. The *areani* having failed to warn, the Wall garrison had been taken unawares, for the local turret and milecastle system of look-out was long out of use [5] as a regular and over-all system and therefore ineffective. The character of the archaeological evidence does not, however, permit any estimate of whether the forts were now deserted or whether their garrisons fell fighting. What is certain is that their buildings were destroyed.

[1] I. A. Richmond, *The Roman Fort at South Shields: a Guide*, 11

[2] XXVII, 8, 10. Denique edictis propositis impunitateque promissa, desertores ad procinctum vocabat et multos alios per diversa libero commeatu dispersos. [3] ibid.

[4] XXVIII, 3, 8. aperte convictos, acceptarum promissarumque magnitudine praedarum allectos, quae apud nos agebantur, aliquotiens barbaris prodidisse.

[5] *CW*[2] XXXIV (1934), 142–3

The new rebuilding is of a remarkable character, hitherto not seen upon the northern frontier. Until this occasion military reconstruction in Northern Britain had everywhere followed the traditional standards of Roman army workmanship, with the result that the masonry and buildings of Constantius I will stand comparison with second-century work. But the new work of A.D. 369 is clumsy botching. Although the stones are set in mortar of good quality they are unsuited for use in regular masonry and would go much better in dry walling. The style may be judged by such work as the repairs to the west wall of Chesterholm [1] or the west guardchamber of the south gate at Birdoswald.[2] It is not the work of trained masons, whether military or civilian; and, if a case were to be made for associating with actual remains the British tradition,[3] that the Wall was built by the provincial *civitates* or tribal *corvées*, it is to this reconstruction, and this alone, that it would be appropriate. The Wall [4] has indeed produced inscriptions of *civitates*, for example, the Dumnonii, the Catuvellauni and the Durotriges Lindinienses, and their lettering, when sophisticated and not clumsy scrawling, would suit this late period better than any other. It is, however, the internal dispositions of the reconstructed forts that make the deeper impression. Even more markedly than the clumsy building, the planning diverges from military tradition. Headquarters buildings [5] came to house granaries, forges or domestic quarters; barracks,[6] smaller than hitherto, witness the breakdown of units, while their contents attest the existence [7] of women, children and sometimes the practice of infanticide.[8] The buildings sprawl everywhere and orderly planning is at

[1] *AA*⁴ VIII (1931), pl. XXXVI, 2 [2] *AA*¹ IV (1855), pl. facing p. 70

[3] C. E. Stevens, *EHR* LVI (1941), 359

[4] *CIL* VII, 775, 776 (Dumnonii), 863 (Catuvellaunii); *EE* VII, 1052; IX, (Durotriges)

[5] Birley, Richmond and Stanfield, *AA*⁴ XIII (1936), 225–7 (granaries, living quarters); *AA*² XXV (1904), 223–5 (forge)

[6] Birley, *AA*⁴ VIII (1931), 195–6

[7] R. C. Bosanquet, *AA*² XXV (1904), 235; cf. 286

[8] Corder, *The Defences of the Roman Fort at Malton*, 67, catalogues 29 such burials

an end. Outside the forts, on the other hand, the civil settlements were not rebuilt, and this point bears forcibly upon the meaning of their new internal arrangements. Civil settlements and forts are in fact merged, and the garrison, if it may be dignified by the name, is no longer a regular unit but a paramilitary community, comprising soldier-settlers and their families, gathered wholly within the protecting ring of the fort walls. They will hold their land by military service, but will also farm it, in a tenure which comes closer to feudal institutions than anything which on the Imperial frontiers had preceded it. It is not first seen in Britain: in North Africa, for example, it had been a commonplace on the Tripolitanian frontier [1] for over a hundred years.

If the general picture of the new age on the Wall is clear, no such clarity yet obtains in the lands behind it. At Piercebridge,[2] for example, the civil-settlement was reconstructed, no doubt because the fort was still held by a regular unit, and until much more is known of forts and their *vici* in the hinterland, it will be impossible to estimate social conditions. This is one of the most interesting of the tasks that face future explorers. In the forward area north of the Wall, however, the outlines of a new state of affairs are apparent, developing from the previous state of affairs, yet fundamentally different from it. It will follow from the new organisation of the Wall garrison, as already described, that the soldier-settlers, deprived of both the *areani* and the outpost forts upon which, like the *exploratores*, they had been based, were no longer expected to take the offensive, and were in fact fundamentally incapable of doing so. The forward territory, so long under Roman military surveillance, could therefore no longer rely upon Roman forces for protection. This explains why it is at this moment that native dynasties emerge in the two traditionally philo-Roman tribes, whose friendly

[1] Goodchild and Ward Perkins, *JRS* XXXIX (1949), 84

[2] G. S. Keeney, *Trans. Architec. & Arch. Soc. Durham & N'b'land,* IX pt. ii. (1941), 135. For a new air-photograph of this settlement, see *JRS* XLV (1955), pl. XVIII.

relations, as Mr Gillam has shown (see pp. 76–7), go back to the second century at least, and begin their pedigrees, as preserved in later Welsh tradition,[1] with chiefs of Roman name, one of whom has a *cognomen*, scarlet-cloak (*pes-rut*), strongly suggestive of Roman investiture. This political phenomenon can be no mere chance. It marks the moment when the tribal chiefs became recognised independent kings, with forces of their own, responsible for holding the northern isthmus. That they would still be in treaty with Rome cannot be doubted: it is the terms of the treaty which had now been significantly revised, in order to concede military power to the natives of an area which Rome had previously undertaken to protect. The new arrangement was clearly of great advantage to the Wall garrison. It is difficult to see how land cultivation could have been possible except under conditions normally peaceful: the sickle and sword cannot be used at once, and by creating the buffer states peace was guaranteed in such a fashion as might make the new military arrangement reasonably sure of success. Socially, it meant that there was now much less difference than ever before between the forward tribes and the Wall garrison, though it must be borne in mind that nothing is known of whence Count Theodosius drew his new *limitanei*. They need not necessarily have been Britons, and could easily have been communities transported *en masse* from Continental frontier areas.

Here may be recalled the vivid picture of such a deportation drawn some fifty years earlier in a panegyric [2] to Constantius Caesar. 'In all the city porticoes sat captive throngs of barbarians; men of astounding wildness afraid, old women and wives despising their sons' or husbands' cowardice, the boys and girls in chains flirting with friendly chatter: all were distributed for duty to your provincials, until they might be taken off to cultivate the wilds for which they were destined. . . . A Chamavan and a Frisian now do my ploughing, and the wandering robber is at work, dirty with country

[1] K. Jackson, *Antiquity* XXIX (1955), 80, takes a conservative view of the matter.
[2] *Pan.* V, 9

toil, and crowds my markets with cattle for sale, while the barbarian crofter pays his tax in kind. Let him be called for conscription, he hastens to be afflicted with duties and burdens, congratulating himself upon the slavery named military service.' This is a graphic impression of the fate which overtook conquered tribes upon unconditional surrender ; and it illustrates well the relief which attended selection for military service rather than serfdom.

The Wall and its forward area were not, however, the only regions reorganised by Count Theodosius. The well-known series of signal-stations on the east coast was now established, and may be brought into connection with a new kind of defence. They are best known [1] upon the cliffs of Yorkshire, from Ravenscar to Filey, and it is likely [2] that they also continued along the cliffs of County Durham. But they are not closely related to important economic areas ; the land behind them, particularly in Yorkshire, was desolate moor, devoid of inhabitants and distant, relatively speaking, from districts which afforded plunder. Their position, watching the sea, is matched by the exactly similar signal-station at Nunnery,[3] upon the island of Alderney, and their purpose was to watch the sea-lanes and to pass messages not inland but laterally, from one to the other. This links them closely in tactical conception with the new naval dispositions described under Valentinian by Vegetius,[4] in which small and swift camouflaged scout-ships were given the task of keeping every raider in sight until the destroyers or *liburnae* could come upon them. Nature gave to the coastal towers, perched on their cliffs, a far more extensive horizon than was visible to any vessel on the ocean surface. The arrangement too would

[1] Collingwood, *Archaeology of Roman Britain* (1930), 57, fig. 13, 60

[2] The most convincing proof so far is the burnt late-Roman masonry used in the early Saxon church at Old Seaham, Co. Durham.

[3] T. D. Kendrick, *The Archaeology of the Channel Islands*, I (1928), 255, fig. 126

[4] *De re mil.* V, 7 scaphae tamen maioribus liburnis exploratoriae sociantur, quae vicenos prope remiges in singulis partibus habeant ; quas Britanni pictas vocant.

indicate that the sea-rovers made their land-fall on the cliffs and then tended to hug the coast, seeking likely landing places and no doubt already knowing, from older hands,[1] the regions productive of good booty. The Yorkshire examples do not stand alone. The Devonshire signal-stations [2] of the same age, differently planned but matched by the late fourth-century post [3] at Barrock Fell (Cumberland), are similarly placed on high cliffs with most unpromising hinterland, and must be taken as similarly related to maritime patrols. These elaborate precautions indicate clearly enough the serious view taken of the sea-raiders, and the measures devised in the west show that Picts and Scots were playing no less harassing a part than Franks or Saxons. The general success of the measures is indicated by the building of a pilgrim shrine on the shores of the Severn estuary at Lydney [4] and the continuing prosperity [5] of the Yorkshire and Rutlandshire *villa*-estates.

In Wales there were some special precautions, related to the copper mines of Anglesey and the Great Orme. The fort at Caernarvon [6] was now rebuilt, and housed a new regiment, whose barracks and headquarters do not reflect at all the same chaotic indiscipline as the buildings of the contemporary Wall-forts. This fort is associated in Welsh legend with Magnus Maximus, Maxsen Gwledig of the Mabinogion [7]

[1] For example, the repeated Scotic raids of Niall, see Ridgway, *JRS* XIV (1924), 131–3. On the terrors of sea-raiding, Amm. Marc. XXVIII, 2, 12 nec quisquam adventum eorum cavere potuit inopinum, non destinata, sed varia petentium et longinqua et quoquo ventus duxerat irrumpentium : quam ob causam prae ceteris hostibus Saxones timentur ut repentini.

[2] Bushe-Fox, *JRS* XXII (1932), 71–2, pl. XIX ; and now in southern Devonshire, St Joseph, *JRS* XLV (1955), pl. XXI, 2

[3] Collingwood, *CW*² XXXI (1931), 111

[4] R. E. M. and T. V. Wheeler, *Report on the Excavation of the Prehistoric, Roman and Post-Roman sites in Lydney Park, Gloucestershire* (1932), 62

[5] Yorkshire : Corder and Kirk, *A Roman Villa at Langton, near Malton, E. Yorkshire* (1932), 62–3 ; Corder, *The Roman Town and Villa at Great Casterton, Rutland, Second Interim Report* (1954), 33

[6] Wheeler, *Segontium and the Roman Occupation of Wales* (1923), 73–89

[7] For English readers the convenient translation is G. Jones and T. Jones, *The Mabinogion*, 79–88 ; for the Welsh text, J. Gwenogvryn Evans, *The White Book Mabinogion* (Pwllheli, 1907).

tale: and while history does not specifically confirm this, Mr C. E. Stevens [1] has pointed out that, in a section of the *Notitia Dignitatum* which is later in date, the *Segontiaci*, surely the men of Segontium, occupy a place suggestive of their having accompanied Maximus in his Continental campaign. Archaeologically, too, the occupation of the fort ends with Maximus, while the legionary fortress at Chester [2] also now ceases to be occupied. If it is thought that these troops, and there must have been many others, were borrowed and expected to return, as in the days of Albinus, there is one argument strongly against such an idea. Their upgrading to the field-army would militate strongly against the likelihood of the demotion which return would imply. Maximus must therefore have made new arrangements or have intended to fill the abandoned posts with new levies as Theodosius must largely have done on the Wall. Here once again native tradition, as Mr C. A. R. Radford has recently observed,[3] appears to come to our aid. The British dynasty of Galloway, whose first ruler, Annwn, bears the Roman name Antonius, traces its descent from Magnus Maximus, in whose interest it was to see the dynasty established. This would mean that Galloway now became a client-kingdom. The other development is the raising of regiments [4] of Atecotti for the Roman army. This would imply that these people were now either reduced to terms or bought over: and, while it might be thought that money and an offer of service would have its effect, the Roman tradition,[5] bare yet unequivocal in statement, that Maximus handled the Picts severely, must not be forgotten. It may well be that he instituted changes of wider import than his hostile historians have seen fit to record.

[1] *Arch. J.* XCVII (1940), 134

[2] C. E. Stevens, *Chester Arch. J.* XXXV (1942), 51: foreshadowed by Wheeler, op. cit., 93, note 75.

[3] MOW Guide, *Whithorn and Kirkmadrine* (1953), 4–5

[4] *Not. Dign. Or.* IX, 29 Atecotti: *Occ.* V, 197 Honoriani Atecotti seniores, 200 iuniores; *Occ.* VII, 78 Atecotti iuniores Gallicani

[5] Prosper Tiro, *Chronicon, Gratiani* IV (A.D. 382), incursantes Pictos et Scotos Maximus strenue superavit.

Maximus perished in 388, and his successors seem to have done little for the northern frontiers. Stilicho's work in the west as described by Claudian [1] is a rehearsal of duties rather than achievements, and there is at least no doubt that his ultimate task was to withdraw troops from Britain [2] in order to defend Rome itself against the incursion of Alaric. After this, between the usurpation of Constantine III and the rescript of Honorius to the tribal communities of Britain, instructing them to take measures for their own safety, there is little to record and certainly no room for reorganisation by a central authority. What is significant is that there was no rapid collapse. Behind the Wall sites continue in occupation well into the fifth century,[3] and even in front of it the coins of Arcadius and Honorius are still circulating at Traprain Law,[4] the key site in the territory of the Votadini, of which so much has been said already. But in North Wales, in relation to which Maximus left gaps in defence, as at Chester and Caernarvon, the Irish [5] began to pour in and settle. This process must have continued for some generations, when the Britons took action. In the second quarter of the fifth century the Votadini from Manau, the district centred about the modern Clackmannan, were persuaded, under their chief Cunedda, to migrate *en masse* to North Wales and to drive out the settlers.[6] That not all the Votadini left is explicitly stated by tradition, but enough came to complete the task and to leave behind them in Anglesey fifth-century memorials, such as the lead coffin from Llangeinwen [7] or the stone of Catumanus the

[1] *I Cons. Stil.* II, 250. Me quoque . . . munivit Stilichon . . . illius effectum curis ne tela timerem Scotica, ne Pictum tremerem, ne litore toto, prospicerem dubiis venturum Saxono ventis.

[2] *De bell. Get.*, 416. venit et extremis legio praetenta Britannis, quae Scoto dat frena truci ferroque notatas, perlegit exsangues Picte moriente figuras.

[3] Collingwood, *JRS* XII (1922), 88–9

[4] See p. 118, note 2: they end with one each of Valens, Valentinian II, and Honorius, three uncertain and one probably of Arcadius.

[5] RCAM, *Anglesey*, xxxvi

[6] Nennius, *Hist. Brit.* 62

[7] RCAM, *Anglesey*, lxxxix; Nash-Williams, *The Early Christian Monuments of Wales* (1950), 59–61

king from Llangadwalader.[1] Although it is alleged by tradition that the Picts now occupied the territory up to the Wall, there is no archaeological support for this, except for the small pockets [2] of Pictish symbol-stones, of which one each exists in Galloway and in Roxburghshire. For the rest the early Christian stones [3] of the two areas tell their own story of Christian Britons, matched by the stone of Brigomaglos from Chesterholm,[4] just south of Hadrian's Wall. Much of the Christian conversion was due to St Ninian of Whithorn, whose activities are now to be fixed[5] in the second quarter of the fifth century, and included the conversion [6] of the Southern Picts of Strathearn and Angus. History in different form had repeated itself.

[1] RCAM, *Anglesey*, civ, 87 ; Nash-Williams, op. cit. 55–7

[2] R. W. Feachem, *PSAS* LXXXIV (1949–50), 206–8. The Whitecleugh chain may be lost and should perhaps be omitted from calculation.

[3] G. Macdonald, *PSAS* LXX (1935–6), 33 ff.

[4] Figured in *An Account of the Roman Antiquities preserved in the Museum at Chesters, Northumberland* (1903), p. 48, no. 247.

[5] C. A. R. Radford and G. Donaldson, MOW Guide, *Whithorn and Kirkmadrine* (1953), 5–6

[6] Bede, *Hist. Eccl.* III, 4

Chapter VI

ANCIENT GEOGRAPHICAL SOURCES FOR BRITAIN NORTH OF CHEVIOT

THE two principal ancient sources for the geography of Britain north of the Cheviot are the geographer Claudius Ptolemaeus [1] and the anonymous compiler of the Ravenna Cosmography.[2] The former, according to ancient tradition,[3] flourished during the principates of Hadrian and Marcus Aurelius : the latter,[4] though working in the sixth century A.D., uses sources of about Ptolemy's period, since he includes the Antonine Wall. Ptolemy, however, does not himself draw upon contemporary sources for his information, though in Britain his latest information, upon the Sixth Legion, cannot be earlier [5] than A.D. 122. His main source was the Trajanic geographer Marinus,[6] whose work he is at pains to criticise, though he obviously used it copiously. So it comes about that much of Ptolemy's information for Britain is in fact the Flavian or even pre-Flavian [7] information available to Marinus. That used for Northern Britain, however, must come from a special source, concerned with North Britain only, since no comparable

[1] *Claudii Ptolemaei Geographia*, ed. C. Müller, Paris (Firmin Didot), 1883. Although a later edition has been published for the maps of the Continent by O. Cuntz, no later edition of the British section is available.

[2] *Ravennatis Anonymi Cosmographia, Itineraria Romana*, II, ed. J. Schnetz (1940). The British section is published, with photographs of the three manuscripts, by I. A. Richmond and O. G. S. Crawford in *Archaeologia* XCIII (1949), 1–50.

[3] *Schedae Savilianae* ; also *Suidas*, s.v., quoted by C. F. A. Nobbe, *Claudii Ptolemaei Geographia*, I, 20

[4] *Archaeologia*, XCIII (1949), 1–2

[5] E. Birley, *Roman Britain and the Roman Army* (1953), 34–5

[6] For Marinus, ibid. : also Honigmann in Pauly-Wissowa, *RE* XIV, 2, 1767–96, who dates his activity to Trajan, but his sources are in doubt earlier.

[7] *Dunium* for the Durotriges appears to be pre-Flavian, see R. E. M. Wheeler, *Reports of the Research Committee of the Society of Antiquaries of London*, XII, *Maiden Castle, Dorset* (1943), 12–13.

information is available for Flavian Wales.[1] Information about the legions in the Welsh border is more up-to-date, for it includes the Twentieth Legion at Chester,[2] posted there not earlier than A.D. 85, and only the similarity of the names *Isca Dumnoniorum* and *Isca Silurum* has introduced confusion about the station of the Second Legion (see below, p. 145). Various layers of information can thus be detected in Ptolemy's British sheet. It is equally clear that not all the information in the Ravenna Cosmography is of the same date: for it includes not only the Antonine Wall, but also the fourth-century title *Augusta* for *Londinium*, and it would seem that the *diversa loca* are an addition from a separate source.

Apart from these, ancient sources are scanty. Epigraphy [3] mentions two place-names and a tribal name. Pliny [4] the elder mentions certain islands and the *Caledonia silva*. Mela [5] mentions the Orkneys, and gets their number right, as does Ptolemy, whether independently or not; but this information may well be derived by both from much older sources, such as Pytheas. Tacitus,[6] who avoids geographical terms, notes north of Cheviot only three, or perhaps four, rivers, the enigmatic *Mons Graupius*, and two district names, while later authors are no less sparing in nomenclature. These subsidiary authorities are therefore mentioned either here or when their names equate with those of the major sources listed below.

[1] The information for Wales includes only two places among the *Ordovices* (II, 3, 18), two among the *Demetae* (II, 3, 23) and one among the *Silures* (II, 3, 24), with no mention of *Venta Silurum*.

[2] II, 3, 19. *Devana, et Legio XX Victrix.*

[3] *CIL* VII 1085 (*Tri*)*monti*; *JRS* XLVII (1957), 230, *castello Veluniate*; *EE* IX, 1005, *Caledo*

[4] *Nat. Hist.* IV, 102, forty *Orcades*, seven *Acmodae*, thirty *Ebudes*; *Mona, Monapia, Riginia, Vectis, Silumnus* and *Andros*; *silva Caledonia*: II, 187, *Camalodunum* (*sic*)

[5] Pomponius Mela, *de Situ Orbis*, III, 6, *triginta sunt Orcades, angustis inter se deductae spatiis, septem Acmodae, contra Germaniam vectae.*

[6] *Agricola*, 22 *Ta*(*na*)*us aestuarium*; 23, *Clota et Bodotria*; the opening sentence of 24 appears to conceal a geographical name; 25, *Caledonia*; 29, *mons Graupius*; 38, *Boresti.*

(i) *The Geography of Ptolemy*

The British Isles form the first sheet [1] in Ptolemy's map of Europe. It is well known that the map of Great Britain, though wonderfully recognisable, is seriously distorted. The cause of this, as Glazebrook Rylands [2] detected, though it led him to calculations which produced results difficult of proof, was twofold. First, there is a constant series of variant readings,[3] which suggest that at a given moment in his work Ptolemy altered the latitude of some of his principal points by half a degree : London and Catterick are notable examples.[4] Secondly, there is the much more important fact that, in dealing with any discrepancy between information based upon measurements by land or sea and observations taken by the gnomon for latitude and lunar eclipse for longitude, Ptolemy, as a professional astronomer, preferred [5] the latter class. But, in view of their relative scarcity, he was compelled to rely largely upon measurements by land and sea, and his map therefore developed what can now be recognised as violent discrepancies, though to him they must have seemed a rational accommodation of two different sets of data. It would therefore not be impossible to correct Ptolemy's map and reduce it to something much more orderly by harmonising the readings of latitude and by removing the discrepancies caused by a clash of terrestrial and astronomical data : and such attempts [6] have been made, both by Rylands and the present writer. But the result is neither Ptolemy nor any version of his work that ever in fact saw the light of day : and, while such processes may assist in identification of his names, it must be realised that the only legitimate treatment of Ptolemy's work is to take it in the state in which he left it, since, whether this represents a final version or a half-finished revision, it

[1] II, 2–3 : cf. VIII, 3
[2] T. G. Rylands, *The Geography of Ptolemy Elucidated*, Dublin, 1893
[3] As between the Thames and London II, 3, 5 and II, 3, 27
[4] See previous note [5] I, 4
[6] Rylands, op. cit. *passim* ; Richmond, *PSAS* LVI (1921–2), 288–301

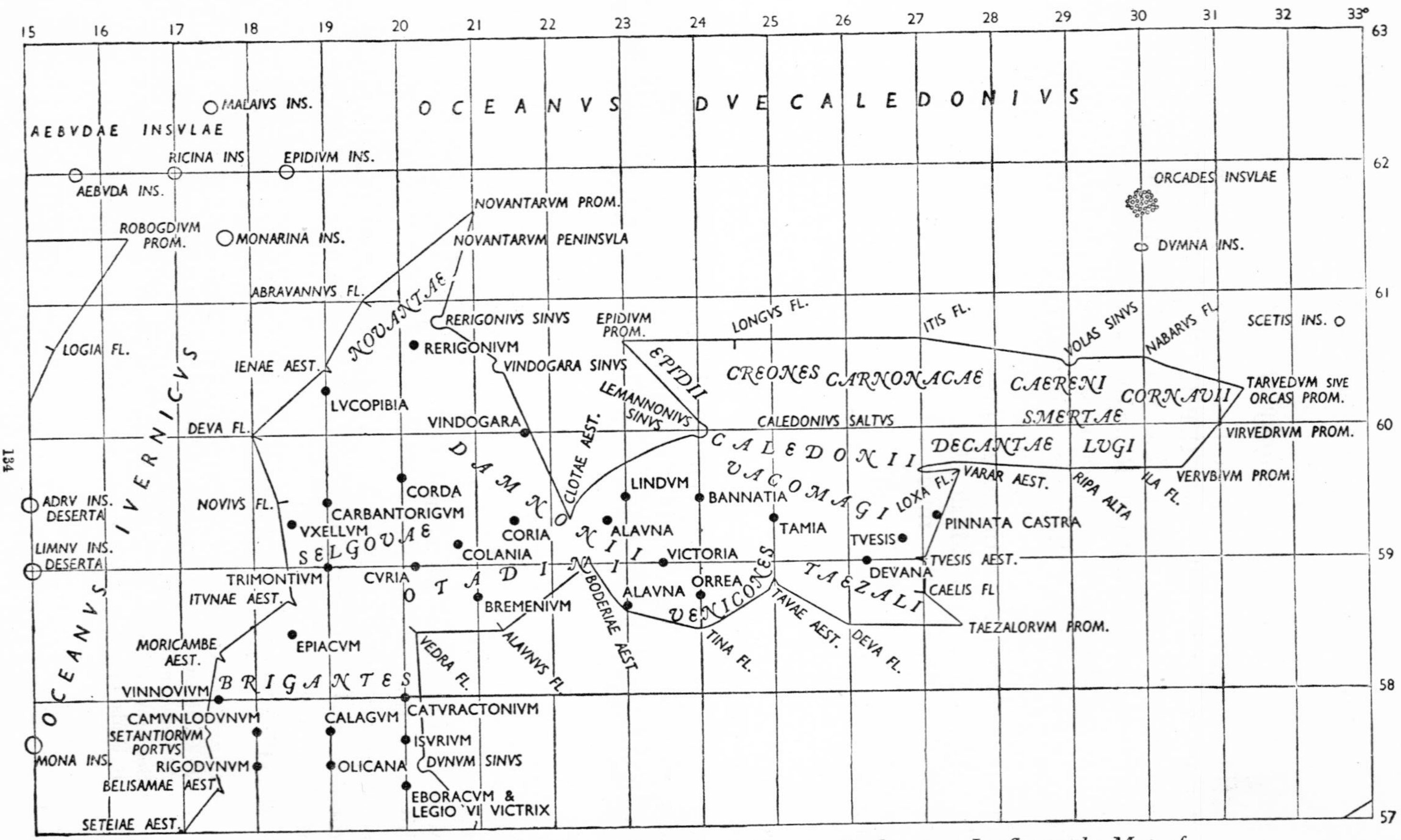

FIG. 6 Ptolemy's Map of Scotland (*Reproduced from the Explanatory Leaflet to the Map of Roman Britain published by the Ordnance Survey*)

is how his work stood at the moment when the task was either considered finished or was laid aside.

In Scotland this line of treatment carries with it important results: for it means that neither latitude nor longitude can be treated seriously, since it is unknown upon what basis of calculation or adjustment either were reached when once the resolve to set the country east and west instead of north and south had been taken. It is also reasonable to take the Latin text as the basis for the names, since both the Greek and Latin versions are of almost equal age and validity.

A useful start can be made from the coastal features, for these sometimes embody tribal names. The identifications of *Novantarum peninsula* and *Novantarum promontorium* as the Rhinns and Mull of Galloway respectively, of *Epidium promontorium* as the Mull of Kintyre, and of *Taezalorum promontorium* as Kinnaird's Head are without question, and carry with them the location of the tribes whose names they bear. Many other names are also easily identified. On the Galloway coast, *Ituna aestuarium*, *Novius* and *Deva* have long been rightly identified respectively with the Eden (or Solway), Nith and Dee. *Iena aestuarium* and *Abravannus* must be equated with Wigtown Bay and the Luce. Between the Rhinns of Galloway and *Clota aestuarium*, the Firth of Clyde, *Rerigonius sinus* and *Rerigonium* go together as Loch Ryan and a place at its head; and *Rerigonium*, whether a Roman fort or native centre, lies behind the Pen Rhionydd [1] of early Welsh poetry. *Vindogara Sinus* and *Vindogara* lie half a degree apart and illustrate well the need for recension which failed to bring them into closer connection. They must be identified with Irvine Bay, and very probably a Roman coastal fort situated upon it and now known to be linked with the inland road-system by way of Loudoun Hill.[2] *Lemannonius Sinus* is difficult to place. Both Loch Long and Loch Fyne have been suggested. It may be remarked, however, that, while in terms of a general survey Loch Fyne is the larger

[1] W. J. Watson, *The History of the Celtic Place-Names of Scotland* (1926), 34
[2] St Joseph in *The Roman Occupation of South-Western Scotland*, 60–5

feature and the more clearly divorced from the Firth of Clyde, the definition of the Caledonii as stretching from the Moray Firth to *Lemannonius sinus* makes Loch Linnhe still more attractive.

Epidium promontorium is the Mull of Kintyre and the *Epidii* are its people. On the other hand, *Epidium insula*, Islay, and *Malaius insula*, Mull, are completely divorced from them and represent features which the change to the east did not carry with it. Similarly the rest of this group of five, known as the *Ebudae*, lie detached and are associated with *Ivernia* (II, 2, 11), but the text correctly states that 'they lie above it,' ὑπέρκεινται, that is, to the north. Their identification is not so certain. There is no agreement upon the two *Ebudae*, or upon the identification of *Ricina* as Rathlin, which the relative positions do not support ; and it would be perhaps more logical to take the two *Ebudae* as Arran and Jura, *Epidium* as Islay, and *Ricina* as Gigha or, if size were the criterion, as Colonsay. *Dumna* and *Scitis*, Lewis and Skye, are clearer, though very ill-placed. The west coast, if Loch Linnhe be regarded as *Lemannonius Sinus*, would be divided between two rivers and a northern gulf, *Volas sinus*, of which the position would suggest Loch Broom. The two rivers in between, in terms of size, might be Loch Sunart (*Longus flumen*) and the Carron (*Itis flumen*). But *Nabarus flumen*, which comes between *Volas sinus* and *Tarvedum sive Orcas promontorium*, must be the Naver ; while *Orcas promontorium* or *Tarvedum*, so manifestly associated with the Orkneys, is surely Dunnet Head. *Orcas promontorium*, like Land's End and the Lizard, has two names in Ptolemy, and, however the southern examples are to be explained, the fact that the name *Orcas* goes back to Pytheas [1] will suggest that he chose the name to associate it directly with the *Orcades*, or Orkney Islands. The second name, *Tarvedum*, may well be the local name, taken from the bull-nose character [2] of Dunnet. The

[1] *Diod. Siculus*. v, 21

[2] Thurso Bay is called Thjórsá, that is, 'Bull's Water,' in Norse, see W. J. Watson, op. cit. 36

other two capes would then be Duncansbay Head (*Virvedrum*) and Noss Head (*Verubium*). This omits Cape Wrath, which now occupies so prominent a place in British geography, but it brings the names into closer contact both with one another and with the closer and more detailed nomenclature of the east coast, and to a point where the transition between neighbouring coasts is much more obvious. To call Cape Wrath *Orcas* would be quite inapposite, since the Orkneys would not be distinguishable at sea-level: at Dunnet they are in immediate view. The relationship of the capes, however, would be much more exact if both *Orcas* and *Virvedrum*, like *Vindogara sinus*, were pulled half a degree farther south.

The East-Coast features now begin. *Ila flumen* is Helmsdale, also known as Strath Ullie or Ilidh. *Ripa alta* is Tarbat Ness. *Varar aestuarium* is the Moray Firth, the name coming from the river Farrar which feeds the innermost Beauly Firth. *Loxa flumen* would be, on present position, the Findhorn: but to move it half a degree southward would bring it to the point occupied by the Lossie, to which it is formally equivalent. *Tuessis flumen* is the Spey, and *Caelis flumen* the Deveron. *Taezalorum promontorium* is Kinnaird's Head. *Deva flumen* is the Aberdeenshire Dee. *Devana*, which takes its name from it, should presumably be pulled half a degree southwards down to its mouth, as in the case of *Vindogara*. Then follow the estuary *Tava*, the river *Tina*, and the estuary *Boderia*. The independent testimony of Tacitus [1] makes it certain that *Boderia* is the Forth. In that case *Tava* and *Tina* must be misplaced, for *Tava* should be the Tay, both by right of name and by right of description as an estuary. But the occurrence of *Tina* in the transposed position would be highly puzzling, since the two likely rivers between Dee and Tay are the North Esk and South Esk, both of which have Celtic names that should have been represented by *Isca*, the well-known British river-name. Here it may be conjectured that the trouble lies not in names but in numbers. The position given

[1] *Agr.* 23

for *Tina* is Lat.—24°, Long.—58° 30′, the latitude being represented in Greek as κ̄δ. If, however, it were κ̄ δ′, the latitude reading would become 20° 15′ and would supply, between Wear (*Vedra*) and Aln (*Alaunus*), the missing river Tyne, which is more important than either. This emendation is at once so necessary and so convincing that it seems worthy of acceptance, ridding Scotland of a puzzle and filling an old-standing gap farther south.

The list of natural features may excite speculation as to whence it came. It is remarkably detailed from Eden to Clyde and from Dunnet Head to Forth or Wear. The west coast, Ptolemy's north coast, is much more sketchily treated, and the amount of material may be compared with the information available for Ireland rather than Great Britain. But even the detailed lists are not without puzzles. On the Galloway coast, Wigtown Bay is treated as an estuary, but why is Luce Bay described as a river ? Has transposition occurred, since in fact Luce Bay is a far larger estuary than Wigtown Bay ? Again, on the east coast why is the Helmsdale river chosen when the Fleet and, in particular, the Oykell are omitted, or in the north-east the Lossie chosen, to the exclusion of the Findhorn or the Ythan ? Farther south, why is the Aln included and the Tweed omitted, although, as Rylands [1] long ago observed, the *Alaunus* in fact occupies the position which should be taken by the Tweed ? Either a detailed list has been copied carelessly, with resultant omissions, or the list has been considered too crowded, and omissions have been made without knowledge of what would have better been retained.

In considering the place-names, their tribal situation must be taken into account. Ptolemy begins with the *Novantae*, whose connection with Wigtownshire has already been noted, and assigns to them *Rerigonium* and *Lucopibia*. The former must be connected with the gulf of the same name. *Lucopibia* is placed between Wigtown Bay and the Dee, which brings the *Novantae* into Kirkcudbrightshire, and if it were pulled half a degree southwards it would be in no bad position for

[1] op. cit. p. 32, pl. XIV

the great Roman fort at Glenlochar. The name is an odd one, and the syllable *pib* is unlikely as a Celtic form, but an emendation does not suggest itself. Next to the *Novantae* and south of them (in reality, east) come the *Selgovae*, with place-names *Carbantorigum*, *Uxellum*, *Corda* and *Trimontium*. The last-named is Newstead, taking its name from the triple peaks of the Eildon, and presumably so named by the Romans, as in Thrace [1]: it takes its place, with *Horrea*, *Victoria* and *Pinnata Castra*, as a name given by the invaders. *Trimontium* occurs at the point where the distortion of Scotland begins, but it does not appear to have been moved. It is correct [2] in relation to Catterick, and the position may have been based upon a bearing. In leaving it where it was Ptolemy arrived at a very odd placing in relation to the known point of *Bremenium*, which has rightly aroused comment, but the explanation appears to lie in the distortion. It is difficult to guess at the other sites, but all are names distinctive of native features: *Uxellum*, 'the lofty,' *Corda*, 'the hosting-place,' and *Carbantoritum*, 'the waggon-ford,' as *Carbantorigum* must surely be emended, speak of native sites rather than Roman, unless they were Roman forts deriving their names, as frequently, from adjacent native centres. If they are in more or less correct relationship to *Trimontium*, which clearly lay upon the eastern fringe, Ptolemy's southern fringe, of the *civitas Selgovarum*, *Uxellum* might be related to Rubers Law, *Carbantoritum* to a point in Teviotdale, and *Corda* to a place in the north-west of the territory, perhaps in the upper Tweed valley. As already observed, *Trimontium* must be in the eastern marches of the *Selgovae*, since it is necessary to allow for the *Otadini* or *Votadini*, whose lands ran coastwise from Tyne to Forth. In their territory two sites are mentioned. The first is *Bremenium*, which is known from two inscriptions to be the fort at High Rochester (Northumberland). The second is *Curia*, 'the host' or 'hosting-place.' It has been suggested that this might be Corbridge, whose name *Corstopitum* is

[1] Pliny, *Nat. Hist.* IV, 41, *urbs a situ Trimontium dicta*

[2] Cf. Rylands, op. cit. pl. XIV, upon which *Trimontium* may be plotted.

usually taken to be corrupt.[1] And if its relationship to *Bremenium* were the criterion, the identification with Corbridge would be supported by it. If, on the other hand, it lay in the northern half of the territory and was related to *Trimontium*, it would lie in the Merse and would suit well enough an identification with Traprain Law. In favour of this interpretation is the likelihood that some place in the northern area of the territory would be mentioned. The fourth Lowland tribe is the *Damnonii*, whose territory runs from Ayrshire by way of Clydesdale and the Midland valley to Stirlingshire and beyond. The Ayrshire *Vindogara* has already been mentioned, as related to Irvine Bay: and the relationship requires adjustment by a half-degree of latitude. This may be compared with the relationship of *Londinium* to the river Thames, of *Vectis* (Isle of Wight) to *Magnus Portus*, and of *Isca Dumnoniorum* to the river Exe, which form certain and indisputable cases, where exactly the same type of correction is required. The next site, *Colania* or *Colanica*, appears to be the same as the *Colanica* of the Ravenna Cosmography, in which it is placed among the Antonine Wall forts. It is there not far east of centre, since the List is now known to run from east to west (see below, p. 147), and as one of the most notable of the Flavian predecessors of the Antonine Wall forts, Castlecary[2] has strong claims to this position. There follow *Coria*, *Alauna*, *Lindum* and *Victoria*, of which the last three are placed by Ptolemy east, in reality, north, of the Forth-Clyde isthmus. *Coria*, however, is situated north of *Colanica*, and all four sites must therefore be connected with Roman forts on the line of penetration northward. If *Alauna* may properly be connected with the river Allen, it might be equated with Ardoch, in which case *Lindum* would be a western outlier, perhaps in the marshy area of the upper Forth, *Victoria* would be Strageath, at the Earn crossing, while

[1] *Northumberland County History*, x, 8–9 : cf. *Archaeologia*, XCIII (1949), 30. *Corso-pitum*, meaning ‘ reedy portion,’ would not be inacceptable.

[2] For Flavian pottery from Castlecary, see G. Macdonald, *Roman Wall in Scotland* (2nd edn. 1934), 250–2.

Coria would be left for the Forth crossing, near Stirling. If the name came from a native *oppidum*, Stirling occupies the key position most likely to provide it.

The tribes of the west coast and far north follow, and it is significant that no place-names are given. Evidently Roman commerce had not made headway in this area of primitive economy,[1] and the place was without principal centres. This would fit the nomadic communities [2] described by Cassius Dio in the Roman north, but in reality applicable only to part of it. The names of the tribes, however, are significant in Celtic,[3] whether related to totems or to economy: the *Epidii* means the 'horse-folk,' the *Cerones* or *Creones*, 'folk of the rough lands,' the *Carnonacae*, the 'folk of the cairns' or 'rocky hills,' the *Caereni* the 'sheep-folk,' and the *Cornavii* the 'folk of the promontory,' as in Cornwall or the Anglesey Llanfihangel-yn-Ngornwy. The *Caledonii* stretch from sea to sea, up the Great Glen. Their forest, Pliny's *silva Caledonia*,[4] is said to be 'above them,' by which Ptolemy means to north, and we to westward. But it would suit the likelihood a good deal better if the text had once read ὑφ' αὐτους instead of ὑπὲρ αὐτους, and the forest had been their foreground rather than their hinterland. Three more tribes follow, the *Decantae*, the *Lugi* and the *Smertae*. The *Decantae*, 'the noble folk,' recall the later Welsh *arx Decantorum*, now Deganwy in Caernarvonshire. If their situation was anything like, Cromarty or the Dornoch peninsula would suit them. The *Lugi*, or 'raven-folk,' could then inhabit the coast between the Dornoch Firth and Helmsdale,

[1] A remarkable picture of primitive Hebridean economy is given in the additions to Solinus, see Mommsen, *C. Iulii Solini collectanea rerum memorabilium* (1864), p. 219, 22, 13–15, incolae nesciunt fruges, piscibus tantum et lacte vivunt. Rex unus est universis, nam quotquot sunt omnes angusta interluvie dividuntur. Rex nihil suum habet, omnia universorum. ad aequitatem certis legibus stringitur ac ne avaritia devertat a vero, discit paupertate iustitiam, utpote cui nihil sit rei familiaris verum alitur e publico. nulla illi femina datur propria sed per vicissitudines in quamcumque commotus sit, usurariam sumit. unde ei nec votum nec spes conceditur liberorum.

[2] Dio, *Hist. Rom.* LXXVI, 12; cf. p. 93, above

[3] W. J. Watson, op. cit., 15–24

[4] Pliny, *Nat. Hist.* IV, 102

for they are described by Ptolemy as in contact with the *Cornavii*. The *Smertae*, whose name suggests the savage custom, attributed to the Irish by Solinus, of smearing themselves with the blood of their enemies, would occupy the hinterland of Ross-shire. Watson has observed [1] that the name survives in *Carn Smeart* (between the Carron and the Oykel).

Below the *Caledonii*—that is, southwards for Ptolemy and eastwards for us—lay the *Vacomagi*. This tribe presents a difficult geographical problem, since it includes places which are situated, according to Ptolemy, as far apart as the Spey valley, with which *Tuessis* must be connected, and *Bannatia*, in the same longitude as the Firth of Tay. While surviving place-names suggest [2] that the *Caledonii* may have ranged from the upper Tay basin to the Moray Firth, it is geographically and historically most unlikely that any tribe could have embraced within its territory both Moray and Strathmore. The more so since the lower Dee valley, which provides the geographical link between them, is assigned by Ptolemy to the *Taezali* of Buchan, in whose territory *Devana* lies. But *Tuessis* might well be a native centre connected with the Spey, in the same way as *Devana* goes with the Dee, while *Pinnata Castra*, which means 'a legionary fortress with merlons,' ought to refer to Inchtuthil.[3] But *Pinnata Castra* is listed (VIII, 3, 9) as one of the four inhabited centres in Britain for which Ptolemy had astronomical bearings, and is therefore by him regarded as a fixed point to which other evidence must somehow be fitted. If, therefore, *Pinnata Castra* were wrongly fixed by observation it would nevertheless remain where it was. The effect would then be that the *Vacomagi* would become extended from Strathmore to Moray because *Pinnata Castra*, really in Strathmore, perforce carried them with it. Some support is lent to this view by the reflection that, if the reverse were the case, and the *Vacomagi* were

[1] op. cit., 17 [2] ibid., 21

[3] This, as Müller perceived, is a better rendering of πτερωτὸν στρατόπεδον (II, 3, 13) than *Alata castra*, meaning equipped with *pinnae*, or merlons, and it agrees with *Pinnatis* of the Ravenna List. The remarkable stone wall round Inchtuthil is exactly suitable.

withdrawn from Strathmore and concentrated in Moray, Strathmore would be empty, whereas it was well known to the Romans and should be comparatively full. On the other hand Moray was much less well known and could very properly be treated in the same fashion as the territory of the *Taezali*, with one river trading-post. Westwards of the *Vacomagi*, or in reality southwards, lay the *Vennicones*, associated with the place-name *Orrea*, the Latin *Horrea*, which Ptolemy fails to aspirate, exactly as in his *Horrea* (*Margi*) in Moesia (III, 9, 5). *Horrea* is placed in the same longitude as the Tay, and its Roman name must identify it as a Roman fort, while its function connects it naturally with sea transport. The Ravenna List (see below, p. 155), specifically names it *Poreo classis*. The large Roman fort at Carpow, on the southern shore of the estuary, will suit the position admirably. *Bannatia* and *Tamia* would then lie westwards (in reality southwards) of *Pinnata Castra*, and, since the word *Bannatia* is connected with a peak, it might be taken as Dealginross, which lies below the native fort on the peak of Dundurn. *Tamia*, on the other hand, is a river-name,[1] and might be linked with the Tay crossing, at its junction with the Almond, which is again the site of a Roman fort.

The sources of Ptolemy's map may thus be put into four categories. Most important to him were the points for which he had bearings. In or near Scotland these [2] are *Caturactonium* (Catterick) and *Eboracum* (York), *Pinnata Castra* (Inchtuthil) and *Dumna* (the island of Lewis). They may be compared with the two other similar points in the island farther south, namely *Londinium* (London) and *Vectis* (Isle of Wight). London, York and Catterick are not so ill related. But the islands are sadly astray, and it may well be the faulty observations for the Isle of Lewis and Inchtuthil together which have caused the distortion of Scotland, as the Isle of Wight has brought distortion to the southern coast of Britain. The second type of source is coastal survey. Good details were plainly available for the whole of the east coast, and for the west

[1] Cf. *Archaeologia*, XCIII (1949), 46, s.v. *Tamion*

[2] VIII, 3, 6–10

coast from Solway (*Ituna aestuarium*) to Clyde (*Clota aestuarium*). Farther north, on the west coast, only the most general information has been employed, and, as with the west coast of Ireland, there is far too little of it to give even an impression of either of these battered and indented shores. In dealing with the material it would appear that Ptolemy may have made a selection, and if it came from Marinus he may have misread some details. As already observed, there are some curious omissions, and it looks as if a misreading accounted for an odd transposition of the Tyne. Two islands have already been noted as the sites of astronomical bearings, but the coastal surveys supplied the names and positions of many more. It is difficult to know whether the very faulty placing in the map is due to Ptolemy or to his sources. The worst cases in the south are Canvey and Sheppey, *Covunnus* and *Toliatis*, which lie far out to sea. But the position given to the southern Hebrides, north of Ireland but far west of Scotland, is relatively no better; and there is much distortion in the positions of Skye, Lewis and the Orkneys, though the estimate of thirty for the last comes very close to the truth. The relationship of the Isle of Wight to *Magnus Portus* is wrong by that half degree of latitude which so frequently upsets relationships in the British sheet.

The third possible source is the Roman itinerary. There can be no doubt that this accounts for such place-names as *Trimontium*, *Victoria*, *Horrea* and *Pinnata Castra*, which are most unlikely to have come from any other source: and with them no doubt went others, such as *Alauna* and *Lindum*, even if it is now impossible to be sure of all. As in all the western provinces and in southern Britain, the names are mostly native place-names taken over, though it is less certain, in so predominantly military an area as Roman Scotland, whether they still represent the same sites. *Trimontium* is an excellent example of the practice by which the place-name applied to a native *oppidum* may be transferred to a purely Roman establishment. The fourth source is that which furnished a list of native places within or outside the Roman sphere of influence. Examples are *Dunium* among the Durotriges, representing Maiden Castle before the Roman town of *Durnovaria* replaced it; *Rigodunum*, *Camulodunum* and the *Dunum* of *Dunum sinus* among the *Brigantes*; or the trading-posts or settlements which derive their names from the rivers at whose mouths they stand, such as *Tamara* and *Uxella* among the *Dumnonii* of Devon, or *Tuessis* and *Devana* in Scotland. The ten native centres of Ireland [1] must have been supplied in the same way, presumably from travellers' records. Upon what basis, when no associated river-name was available, Ptolemy gave them a position cannot now be determined. But the ingenuity which made a place-name [2] out of a phrase in Tacitus, *ad sua tutanda*, was not incapable of inventing a position for a non-existent feature, and this point must not be forgotten. It seems certain that in Britain a confusion between *Isca Dumnoniorum* and *Isca Silurum* led Ptolemy to misplace the *castra* of the Second Legion, and to associate it with Exeter. It will be observed that he does not give the two points the same reading; they vary by ten minutes of latitude, which suggests that Ptolemy may have had before him in his source another numeral for the degrees. But if he did not know that *Isca* lay among the *Silures*—and his information upon the legions may well have come from a source which specified no tribal name—he would have felt compelled to connect the legion with the only *Isca* which he knew, among the *Dumnonii*. The difficulty which similar names presented to the ancient geographer is well illustrated by Ptolemy's own comment (I, 15, 6) upon Marinus, who, while 'saying that *Noviomagus* is 59 miles south-west of London, shows it to the north in his bearings.' Where the northward *Noviomagus* of Marinus lay is not now apparent, unless it was the original name for *Caesaromagus* [3] among the Trinovantes. The south-westward position is correct for *Noviomagus Regnensium*, now Chichester, and is correctly given to it by

[1] II, 2, 4–10 [2] II, 11, 27: cf. Tac. *Ann.* IV, 73

[3] For *Caesaromagus*, see *It. Ant.* 474, 3, 480, 6; also C. E. Stevens, *EHR* LII (1937), 198

Ptolemy. The confusion of the two places named *Isca* is, on the contrary, wrongly resolved by Ptolemy, and well illustrates the manner in which may have arisen the difficulty in Scotland noted above, which gives positions in the Spey and the Tay valleys to the same tribe. Yet, despite all mistakes and difficulties Ptolemy must be accorded high praise for so good a map of the British Isles when the quality of his work is weighed against the amount of information available. He was in fact attempting too much upon too narrow a basis.

(ii) *The Antonine Itinerary*

The second source for the ancient geography of Scotland is a short one. The Antonine Itinerary,[1] compiled under Caracalla between 212 and 216, and revised in the fourth century, touches the area at two points only. The outpost forts of Hadrian's Wall at *Castra Exploratorum* (Netherby) and *Blatobulgium* (Birrens) occur in *Iter* II of the British List: while that at *Bremenium* (High Rochester) occurs in *Iter* I. The mileage associated with them is not quite correct. *Bremenium* is 25 Roman miles from *Corstopitum* (Corbridge), whereas the Itinerary gives it as 20: *Castra Exploratorum* is 11 Roman miles from *Luguvalium* (Carlisle), while the Itinerary gives 12; and *Blatobulgium* is 14 from *Castra Exploratorum*, 2 miles longer than the Itinerary's 12. The latter pair of discrepancies is not large. In the former case, a Roman figure five may have dropped from the numeral. Among the names only *Bremenium* is mentioned by Ptolemy. The other two occur in the Itinerary alone.

(iii) *The Ravenna Cosmography*

The third geographical source for the ancient place-names of Scotland is the Ravenna Cosmography,[2] a list of places in

[1] O. Cuntz, *Itineraria Antonini Augusti et Burdigalense, Itineraria Romana*, I (Leipzig, 1929)

[2] *Archaeologia*, XCIII (1949), 1–50: cf. J. Schnetz, *Ravennatis anonymi cosmographia, Itineraria Romana*, II (Leipzig, 1939), also Pinder and Parthey, *Ravennatis anonymi cosmographia* (Berlin, 1860)

Britain and the whole Roman world compiled during the seventh century at Ravenna. It has been shown [1] that it mainly derives from a road map of the kind exemplified by the Peutinger Table,[2] a medieval copy of a map of the late-Roman Empire, based upon itineraries and marking the roads. For large portions of Roman Britain the connection with a road map has been clearly demonstrated, and has been shown to extend into Scotland. The chief difficulty of interpretation is, however, that there is hardly ever a break in the list of names indicative of a change of route. Further, the demonstrable habit of the work [3] is to take roads radiating from a given centre without quoting the name of the centre more than once. Much independent knowledge of the road system and of the associated ancient names is accordingly required for the interpretation of the list, and this is exactly what is lacking in Scotland. As to date, the work appears to be virtually contemporary with Ptolemy: but, while Ptolemy derived his material for Britain largely from first-century sources, the material upon which the Ravenna List is based includes the Antonine Wall, treating it, like Hadrian's Wall, from east to west, as is demonstrated by a newly discovered inscription [4] identifying *Veluniate*, the *Velunia* of the Ravennas, with Carriden. By comparison, then, it is possible to recognise in the middle of the list north of Hadrian's Wall five names associated with Dere Street, from Newstead (*Trimontium*) southwards: *Trimontium*, which is Newstead itself, *Eburocaslum*, probably Cappuck, *Bremenium*, known from inscriptions [5] to be High Rochester, a site on the Coquet named *Coccuveda*, and another on the Aln, named *Alauna*. The three following names are obscure and probably corrupt. If *Eiudensca* had anything to do with the *Urbs Giudi* [6] of Bede, it might be Inveresk. *Olcaclavis*,[7] the place between it and

[1] *Archaeologia* XCIII (1949), 4–5 [2] ibid. pl. I [3] ibid. 6–12

[4] *JRS* XLVII (1957), 230; I owe advance information of this valuable stone to the kindness of Mr R. B. K. Stevenson and Dr K. A. Steer.

[5] *CIL* VII, 1030, 1037

[6] Bede, *Hist. Eccl.*, I, 12, *orientalis (sinus) habet in medio sui urbem Giudi.*

[7] *Archaeologia*, XCIII (1949), 42

Trimontium, would then be the lost site at Crichton, and is connected with a Celtic word *olca*, 'a meadow,' the basis of the Old French *ouche*. *Rumabo* defies analysis. The list is then divided by the Antonine Wall, upon which ten forts (or eleven if *Medio-nemeton* were two names fused) are named out of nineteen. This is a very possible curtailment if the original source was an Itinerary and the numerous smaller forts were omitted.[1] But identifications are difficult and, as already observed, perhaps the most likely is that of Ptolemy's *Colanica* as Castlecary, where a quantity of Flavian pottery [2] attests a substantial pre-Antonine occupation. The twenty-seven names which follow include five placed by Ptolemy north of the isthmus, while in the south, among the twenty-six names preceding *Trimontium*, three names also noted by Ptolemy are to be discussed. They are, in the north, *Pinnatis*, *Tuessis*, *Devoni*, *Poreo classis* (for *Horrea classis*) and *Victoria*. The southern three are *Uxela*, *Corda* and *Carbant(or)i(t)um*. If the identity of the names *Smetriadum* and *Smetri* were sure, we should probably have here a road junction, with branches to *Carbant(or)i(tum)* and to *Uxela* and/or *Corda* respectively. But in default of identifiable names no progress can be made in this direction.

There follows, however, a remarkable section, introduced, quite differently from all others, by the words *sunt autem in ipsa Britan(n)ia diversa loca, ex quibus aliquanta nominare volumus*. Then follow the names *Maponi*, *Mixa*, *Panovius*, *Minox*, *Taba*, *Manavi*, *Segloes* and *Dannoni*. These eight are evidently drawn from a separate source, not an itinerary, and the last four have strong Scottish associations (Fig. 2, p. 98). *Taba*, for *Tava*, can be linked with the Tay, and *Manavi* with the district of *Manau*, between the Carron and the Forth. *Segloes*, corrupted for *Selgo(v)e(n)s(is)*, is the adjective formed from the tribal name of the *Selgovae*, and *Dannoni* goes with the *Damnonii*. Further, the first four names begin with *Maponi*, connected, as the late Professor W. J. Watson [3] observed,

[1] Cf. the treatment of Hadrian's Wall, ibid. 13

[2] See p. 140 note 2 [3] op. cit., 181

with the god *Maponus* and the Dumfriesshire names of Clochmabenstane, an ancient Border trysting-spot, and Lochmaben. The reason for the separation of this part of the list now becomes apparent. The source is not an Itinerary, but a list of tribal meeting-places, or *loca*, whose existence and use was officially recognised by Rome. The date of this part of the list is not easy to fix ; but parallel arrangements on the Danube [1] belong to areas evacuated by Rome yet still subject to treaty regulation and surveillance, and this suits the third or even the fourth century rather than the second. It is thus possible that this part of the List affords a glimpse of the state of affairs in Scotland after Caracalla, when the tribes from the Tay to the Roman border were in treaty-relation with Rome, and may well have had their fixed places of assembly and commerce. Had the list belonged to an earlier period, when the Romans were in full possession of the land, the places should have been fitted in with the rest of the information belonging to that time which the List affords.

The List also gives a number of rivers. But most of these do not belong to Scotland. The only certain instance appears to be the *Anava*, which follows the Cumberland Derwent and may be identified [2] with the Annan. But an East-Coast list begins with *Bdora*, which may well be a corruption for *Bodotria* or *Boderia*, the names accorded by Tacitus and Ptolemy respectively to the Forth.

[1] Dio, LXXI, 15, LXXII, 2 (Marcomanni) ; LXXI, 19 (Iazyges) ; LXXII, 3 (Buri)
[2] *Archaeologia*, XCIII (1949), 22

APPENDIX: THE SOURCES

I. Ptolemy's Geography : Extracts relating to Britain North of the Cheviot

(i) The Coastal Features

(*a*) II, 2, 11

The islands called *Ebudae* lie north of Ireland, five in number. The westernmost of them is called

	Lat.	Long.
Ebuda	15° 00′	62° 00′

and the next of them lies similarly towards the east.

Ebuda	15° 40′	62° 00′
Ricina	17° 00′	62° 00′
Maleus	17° 30′	62° 30′
Epidium	18° 30′	62° 00′

(*b*) II, 3, 1

The outline of the north side of the British island Albion, above which lies the ocean called Duecaledonian :

	Lat.	Long.
Novantarum peninsula et Novantarum promontorium	21° 00′	61° 40′
Rerigonius sinus	20° 30′	60° 50′
Vindogara sinus	21° 20′	60° 30′
Clotae aestuarium	22° 15′	59° 20′
Lemannonius sinus	24° 00′	60° 00′
Epidium promontorium	23° 00′	60° 40′
Longi fluminis ostia	24° 30′	60° 40′
Ityi fluminis ostia	27° 00′	60° 40′

	Lat.	*Long.*
Volas sinus	29° 00′	60° 30′
Nabari fluminis ostia	30° 00′	60° 30′
Tarvedum sive Orcas promontorium	31° 20′	60° 15′

(*c*) II, 3, 2

The outline of the western side, which lies over against the Hibernian Ocean and the Vergionian Ocean, following *Novantarum peninsula*:

	Lat.	*Long.*
Abravanni fluminis ostia	19° 20′	61° 00′
Ienae aestuarium	19° 00′	60° 30′
Devae fluminis ostia	18° 00′	60° 00′
Novii fluminis ostia	18° 20′	59° 30′
Itunae aestuarium	18° 30′	58° 45′

(*d*) II, 3, 5

The outline of the eastward and southward sides, over against the German Ocean. After *Tarvedum sive Orcas promontorium*, as it is called,

	Lat.	*Long.*
Virvedrum promontorium	31° 00′	60° 00′
Verubium promontorium	30° 30′	59° 40′
Ilae fluminis ostia	30° 00′	59° 40′
Ripa alta	29° 00′	59° 40′
Loxae fluminis ostia	27° 30′	59° 40′
Varar aestuarium	27° 00′	59° 40′
Tuessis aestuarium	27° 00′	59° 00′
Celnii fluminis ostia	27° 00′	58° 45′
Taezalorum promontorium	27° 30′	58° 30′
Devae fluminis ostia	26° 00′	58° 30′
Tavae aestuarium	25° 00′	58° 50′
Tinae fluminis ostia	24° 00′	58° 30′

	Lat.	Long.
Boderiae aestuarium	22° 30′	59° 00′
Alauni fluminis ostia	21° 00′	58° 30′
Vedrae fluminis ostia	20° 10′	58° 30′

(ii) The Tribes and their Settlements

II, 3, 7

The *Novantae* inhabit the lands along the north side, below the peninsula bearing their name. Here there are the following towns:

	Lat.	Long.
Lucopibia	19° 00′	60° 20′
Rerigonium	20° 10′	60° 40′

8. Below them the *Selgovae*, in whose lands are the following towns:

	Lat.	Long.
Carbantorigum	19° 00′	59° 30′
Uxellum	18° 30′	59° 20′
Corda	20° 00′	59° 40′
Trimontium	19° 00′	59° 00′

9. East of these and more northerly the *Damnonii*, in whose lands are the following towns:

	Lat.	Long.
Colanica	20° 45′	59° 10′
Vindogara	21° 20′	60° 00′
Coria	21° 30′	59° 20′
Alauna	22° 45′	59° 50′
Lindum	23° 00′	59° 30′
Victoria	23° 30′	59° 00′

10. The *Otadini* farther south, in whose lands are the following towns:

	Lat.	*Long.*
Curia	20° 10′	59° 00′
Alauna	23° 00′	58° 40′
Bremenium	21° 00′	58° 45′

11. After the *Damnonii* towards the east but farther north, from *Epidium promontorium* eastwards, the *Epidii*, after these the [*Cerones*, then farther eastwards, the] *Creones*; then the *Carnonacae*, then the *Caereni*, and, farther eastwards at the end, the *Cornavii*.

12. From the *Lemannonius sinus* to *Varar aestuarium* the *Caledonii*, and beyond them *Caledonia silva*; east of them the *Decantae*, after which the *Lugi*, bounding the *Cornavii*, and, beyond the *Lugi*, the *Smertae*.

13. Beyond the *Caledonii* the *Vacomagi*, where there are the following towns:

	Lat.	*Long.*
Bannatia	24° 00′	59° 30′
Tamia	25° 00′	59° 20′
Pinnata castra	27° 15′	59° 20′
Tuessis	26° 45′	59° 10′

14. Below these, but more westerly, the *Venicones*, where there is a town:

	Lat.	*Long.*
Horrea	24° 00′	58° 45′

15. More easterly the *Taexali* and the town:

	Lat.	*Long.*
Devana	26° 15′	59° 00′

II. The Antonine Itinerary

(*a*) [Iter I.]

A limite, id est a vallo, Praetorio usque, m.p.m.	clvi
A Bremenio Corstopitum	xx

(*b*) [Iter II.]

Item a vallo ad portum Ritupis m.p.m.	cccclxxxi
A Blatobulgio Castra Exploratorum	xii
Luguvallo	xii

III. The Ravenna Cosmography

(*a*) The Lowlands, from the south-west to Newstead, 156–83

Brocara, Croucingo, Stodoion, Smetriadum, Clindum, Carbantium, Tadoriton, Maporiton, Alitacenon, Loxa, Locatreve, Cambroianna, Smetri, Uxela, Lucotion, Corda, Camulosessa, Presidium, Brigomono, Abisson, Ebio, Coritiotar, Celovion, Itucodon, Maromago, Duabsissis, Venutio, Trimuntium.

(*b*) From Newstead across the Cheviot, 184–90

Eburocaslum, Bremenium, Coccuveda, Alauna, Olcaclavis, Eiudensca, Rumabo.

(*c*) The Antonine Wall, from east to west, 191–200

Iterum sunt civitates in ipsa Britan(n)ia recto tramite una alteri connexae, ubi et ipsa Britan(n)ia plus angustissima de oceano in oceanum esse dinoscitur. Id est : Velunia, Volitanio, Pexa, Begesse, Colanica, Medionemeton, Subdobiadon, Litana, Cibra, Credigone.

(*d*) North of the Antonine Wall, 201–27

Iterum est civitas quae dicitur : Lano, Maulion, Demerosessa, Cindocellum, Cerma, Veromo, Matovion, Ugrulentum, Ravatonium, Iberran, Pinnatis, Tuessis, Lodone, Litinomago, Devoni, Memanturum, Decha, Bograndium, Ugueste, Leviodanum, Poreo classis, Levioxava, Cermium, Victorie, Marcotaxon, Tagea, Voran.

(*e*) Various Places, 228–35

Sunt autem in ipsa Britan(n)ia diversa loca, ex quibus aliquanta nominare volumus. Id est : Maponi, Mixa, Panovius, Minox, Taba, Manavi, Segloes, Dannoni.

(*f*) Rivers

Currunt autem per ipsam Britan(n)iam plurima flumina, ex quibus aliquanta nominare volumus. Id est :

251 *Anava*
252 *Bdora*

BIBLIOGRAPHY AND ABBREVIATIONS

*AA*1–4 *Archaeologia Aeliana*, Newcastle-upon-Tyne ; first to fourth series

Alföldi, A. 'The Moral Barrier of Rhine and Danube,' *Congress of Roman Frontier Studies 1949* (Durham 1952), 1–16

Ant. J. *The Antiquaries Journal*, London

Arch. J. *The Archaeological Journal*, London

Arnold, W. T. *Studies of Roman Imperialism*, ed. E. Fiddes, Manchester 1906

Beardsley, R. K. 'Hypotheses on Inner Asian Pastoral Nomadism and its Cultural Areas,' *Mem. Soc. Amer. Arch.* IX (supplement to *Amer. Antiquity* XVIII), 24–8 (Utah 1953)

Bersu, G. 'Excavations at Little Woodbury, Wiltshire—Part I: The Settlement as revealed by excavation,' *PPS* VI (1940), 30–111

'Rectangular Enclosure on Green Craig, Fife,' *PSAS* LXXXII (1947–8), 264–75

Birley, E. 'An Introduction to the Excavations of Chesterholm-Vindolanda,' *AA*4 VIII (1931), 182–212

'Materials for the History of Roman Brougham,' *CW*2 XXXII (1932), 124–39

'Fifth Report on the Excavations at Housesteads,' *AA*4 XIV (1937), 172–84

'Excavations at Birrens 1936–7,' *PSAS* LXXII (1937–8), 275–347

'Roman Inscriptions from Chesters,' *AA*4 XVI (1939), 237–51

'The Beaumont Inscription, the Notitia Dignitatum and the Garrison of Hadrian's Wall,' *CW*2 XXXIX (1939), 190–226

'Noricum, Britain and the Roman Army,' *Beiträge zur älteren Europäischen Kulturgeschichte für Rudolf Egger* I, Klagenfurt 1952–3, 175–88

Roman Britain and the Roman Army, Kendal 1953

'The Roman fort at Netherby,' *CW*2 LIII (1953), 6–39

Birley, E., Charlton, J. and Hedley, P. 'Excavations at Housesteads in 1931,' *AA*4 IX (1932), 222–37

'Excavations at Housesteads in 1932,' *AA*4 X (1933), 82–96

Birley, E. and Keeney, G. S. 'Fourth Report on Excavations at Housesteads,' *AA*4 XII (1935), 204–58

Birley, E., Richmond, I. A. and Stanfield, J. A. 'Excavations at Chesterholm-Vindolanda: Third Report,' *AA*4 XIII (1936), 218–57

Bosanquet, R. C. 'Excavating on the line of the Roman Wall in Northumberland—The Roman Camp at Housesteads,' *AA*2 XXV (1904), 193–299

Bowen, Collin 'The Problem of Roman Villa Fields,' *Arch. News-Letter* VI no. 2 (1955), 35–40

Brailsford, J. W. 'Excavations at Little Woodbury (1938–9), Part II,' *PPS* XIV (1948), 1–23

'Excavations at Little Woodbury,' *PPS* XV (1949), 156–68

Brogan, Olwen 'Trade between the Roman Empire and free Germans,' *JRS* XXVI (1936), 195–222

Bruce, J. C. *Handbook to the Roman Wall*, 10th ed., Newcastle 1947

Bruns, Carl E. Georg *Fontes Juris Romani*, 7th ed., Tübingen 1909

Bushe-Fox, J. P. 'The Use of Samian Pottery in dating the early Roman occupation of the north of Britain,' *Archaeologia* LXIV (1912–13), 295–314

'Some Notes on Coast Defences,' *JRS* XXII (1932), 60–72 and plates

CAH *Cambridge Ancient History*

Callander, J. Graham 'Notice of the Discovery of Two Vessels of Clay on the Culbin Sands,' *PSAS* XLV (1910–11), 158–81

Casson, T. E. 'Cartimandua, in history, legend and romance,' *CW*² XLIV (1944), 68–80

Cheesman, G. L. *The Auxilia of the Roman Imperial Army*, Oxford 1914

Childe, V. G. *Prehistoric Communities of the British Isles*, Edinburgh 1940

Scotland before the Scots, London 1946

Christison, D., Barbour, J. and Anderson, J. 'An Account of the Excavation of the Camps and Earthworks of Birrenswark Hill in Annandale, undertaken by the Society in 1898,' *PSAS* XXXIII (1898–9), 198–249

Cichorius, Conrad *Die Reliefs der Traians-säule*, Berlin 1896–1900

CIL *Corpus Inscriptionum Latinarum*, Berlin 1863

Clark, J. G. D. 'Report on Excavations on the Cambridgeshire Car Dyke, 1947,' *Ant.J.* XXIX (1949), 145–63

Clarke, J. *The Roman Fort at Cadder*, Glasgow 1933

'Excavations at Milton (Tassiesholm) in season 1950,' *Trans. Dum. & Gall. Ant. & Nat. Hist. Soc.* XXVIII (1949–50), 199–221

Clarke, J. and Webster, A. B. 'Corbridge: Interim Report, 1953–4,' *Trans. Dum. & Gall. Ant. & Nat. Hist. Soc.* XXXII (1953–4), 9–34

Collingwood, R. G. 'The Roman Evacuation of Britain,' *JRS* XII (1922), 74–98

'Town and Country in Roman Britain,' *Antiquity* III (1929), 261–76

The Archaeology of Roman Britain, London 1930

'A Roman fortlet on Barrock Fell near Low Hesket,' *CW*² XXXI (1931), 111–18

'The Hill-Fort on Carrock Fell,' *CW*² XXXVIII (1938), 32–41

Collingwood, R. G. and Myres, J. N. L. *Roman Britain and the English Settlements*, 2nd ed., Oxford 1937

Corder, P. *The Roman Town and Villa at Great Casterton, Rutland, Second Interim Report*, Nottingham 1954

'The Reorganisation of the Defences of Romano-British Towns in the Fourth Century,' *Arch.J.* CXII (1955), 20–42

Corder, P. and Davies Pryce, T. 'Belgic and other pottery found at Ferriby. With comments on pre-Claudian Romano-Gaulish influence in Britain,' *Ant.J.* XVIII (1938), 262–77

Corder, P. and Kirk, J. L. *A Roman Villa at Langton, near Malton, E. Yorkshire*, Leeds 1932

Corder, P., Mattingly, H. and Hull, M. R. *The Defences of the Roman Fort at Malton*, Leeds n.d.

Crawford, O. G. S. *The Topography of Roman Scotland, North of the Antonine Wall*, Cambridge 1949
CRFS *Congress of Roman Frontier Studies 1949*, Durham
Cross, T. P. and Slover, C. H. *Ancient Irish Tales*, New York 1935
Cuntz, O. (ed.) *Itineraria Antonini Augusti et Burdigalense*, *Itineraria Romana* I, Leipzig 1929
Curle, A. O. 'Account of Excavations on Traprain Law in the Parish of Prestonkirk, County of Haddington, in 1914,' *PSAS* XLIX (1914–15), 139–202
Curle, A. O. and Cree, J. E. 'Account of the Excavation on Traprain Law during the summer of 1920,' *PSAS* LV (1920–1), 153–206
'Account of the Excavations on Traprain Law during the summer of 1921,' *PSAS* LVI (1921–2), 189–259
Curle, J. *A Roman frontier Post and its People*, Glasgow 1911
'An Inventory of Objects of Roman and Provincial Roman Origin found on Sites in Scotland not definitely associated with Roman Constructions,' *PSAS* LXVI (1931–2), 277–400
Curwen, E. C. 'Ancient Cultivations at Grassington, Yorkshire,' *Antiquity* II (1928), 168–72
'Ancient Cultivations,' *Antiquity* VI (1932), 389–406
'Early Development of Agriculture in Britain,' *PPS* IV (1938), 27–51
*CW*² *Transactions of the Cumberland and Westmorland Antiquarian and Archaeological Society*, new series
Davies, O. *Roman Mines in Europe*, Oxford 1935
Davies Pryce, T. and Birley, E. 'The fate of Agricola's Northern Conquests,' *JRS* XXVIII (1938), 141–52
Domaszewski, Alfred von *Die Rangordnung des römischen Heeres*, Bonn 1908
EE *Ephemeris Epigrapha*, Berlin 1872–1905
Elgee, F. *Early Man in North-East Yorkshire*, Gloucester 1930
Evans, J. Gwenogvryn *The White Book Mabinogion*, Pwllheli 1907
Fairhurst, H. and Scott, J. G. 'The Earthwork at Camphill in Glasgow,' *PSAS* LXXXV (1950–1), 146–57
Feachem, R. W. 'A new Pictish symbol-stone in the Lowlands,' *PSAS* LXXXIV (1949–50), 206–8
Fox, Aileen 'Hill-Slope Forts and Related Earthworks in SW. England and South Wales,' *Arch.J.* CIX (1952), 1–22
Fox, Sir Cyril *The Personality of Britain*, 4th ed., Cardiff 1943
A find of the Early Iron Age from Llyn Cerrig Bach, Cardiff 1946
Gibson, J. P. and Simpson, F. G. 'The Milecastle on the Wall of Hadrian at the Poltross Burn,' *CW*² XI (1911), 390–441
Gillam, J. P. 'Calpurnius Agricola and the northern frontier,' *Trans. Architec. & Arch. Soc. Durham & N'b'land* X, pt iv (1953), 359–75
Goodchild, R. G. 'T-shaped Corn drying Ovens in Roman Britain,' *Ant.J.* XXIII (1943), 148–53
Goodchild, R. G. and Ward Perkins, J. B. 'The *Limes Tripolitanus* in the Light of Recent Discoveries,' *JRS* XXXIX (1949), 81–95
Gowland, W. 'The Early Metallurgy of Silver and Lead—Part I: Lead,' *Archaeologia* LVII (1901), 359–422
Green, C. 'Glevum and the Second Legion,' *JRS* XXXII (1942), 39–47

Grenier, A. in *Manuel d'Archéologie préhistorique celtique et gallo-romaine*, ed. J. Déchelette, Paris 1908–34

Grimes, W. F. 'The Jurassic Way across England,' in *Aspects of Archaeology in Britain and Beyond*, London 1951

Haverfield, F. 'Modius Claytonensis: the Roman Bronze Measure from Carvoran,' *AA*[3] XIII (1916), 85–102

Hawkes, C. F. C. 'Britons, Romans and Saxons round Salisbury and in Cranborne Chase,' *Arch.J.* CIV (1947), 27–81

Hawkes, C. F. C. and J. J. *Prehistoric Britain*, London 1947

Hawkes, C. F. C. and Hull, M. R. *Camulodunum*, London 1947

Helbaek, H. 'Early Crops in Southern England,' *PPS* XVIII (1952), 194–233

Henshall, Audrey S. 'Textiles and Weaving Appliances in Prehistoric Britain,' *PPS* XVI (1950), 130–62

Hogg, A. H. A. 'Native Settlements of Northumberland,' *Antiquity* XVII (1943), 136–47

'A New list of the Native Sites of Northumberland,' *PSAN*[4] XI (1946–50), 140–79

'The Votadini,' in *Aspects of Archaeology in Britain and Beyond*, London 1951

Holleyman, G. A. 'The Celtic Field-System in South Britain: a survey of the Brighton District,' *Antiquity* IX (1935), 443–54

ILS *Inscriptiones Latinae Selectae*

Jackson, K. 'The Britons in Southern Scotland,' *Antiquity* XXIX (1955), 77–88

Jessen, K. and Helbaek, H. *Cereals in Great Britain and Ireland in Prehistoric and Early Historic Times*, Copenhagen 1944

Jones, G. and T. *The Mabinogion*, London 1949

JRS *Journal of Roman Studies*, London

Keeney, G. S. 'Excavations at the Roman site at Piercebridge in 1938,' *Trans. Architec. & Arch. Soc. Durham & N'b'land* IX, pt i (1939), 43–68

'Excavations at the Roman fort of Piercebridge in 1939,' *ibid.* IX, pt ii (1941), 127–38

'Excavations at the Roman fort at Piercebridge in 1948 and 1949,' *ibid.* X, pt iii (1950), 285–309

Kendrick, T. D. *The Archaeology of the Channel Islands* I, London 1928

Kilbride-Jones, H. E. 'An Aberdeenshire Iron-Age Miscellany,' *PSAS* LXIX (1934–5), 445–54

'The Excavation of a native settlement at Milking Gap, High Shield, Northumberland,' *AA*[4] XV (1938), 303–50

Kitson Clarke, Mary 'Where were the Brigantes?' *YAJ* XXXIV (1938), 80–7

Kornemann, Ernst *Weltgeschichte des Mittelmeerraumes* II, Munich 1949

Leeds, E. T. *Celtic Ornament in the British Isles down to A.D. 700*, Oxford 1933

Macdonald, Sir George 'The Agricolan Occupation of North Britain,' *JRS* IX (1919), 111–38

'A Roman Inscription found at Jedburgh, and some Roman Sculptures recently presented to the National Museum,' *PSAS* LVII (1922–3), 173–80

'Roman Coins found in Scotland—II,' *PSAS* LVIII (1923–4), 325–9
The Roman Wall in Scotland, 2nd ed., Oxford 1934
'The dating-value of Samian ware: a rejoinder,' *JRS* XXV (1935), 187–200
'On two Inscribed Stones of the Early Christian Period from the Border District,' *PSAS* LXX (1935–6), 33–9
'Britannia Statim Omissa,' *JRS* XXVII (1937), 93–8
'Verbum non amplius addam,' *JRS* XXIX (1939), 5–27

May, T. 'The Roman Forts at Elslack,' *YAJ* XXI (1910–11), 113–67

Miller, S. N. 'Roman York: excavations of 1926–7,' *JRS* XVIII (1928), 61–99
'An Historical Survey,' in *The Roman Occupation of SW. Scotland*, Glasgow 1952

Momigliano, A. '*Panegyricus Messallae* and "Panegyricus Vespasiani,"' *JRS* XL (1950), 41–2

Morris, John 'The Vallum again,' *CW*² L (1950), 43–53

Mortimer, J. R. *Forty Years' Researches in British and Saxon burial mounds of East Yorkshire*, London n.d.

Müller, C. (ed.) *Claudii Ptolemaei Geographia*, Paris 1883

Nash-Williams, V. E. *The Early Christian Monuments of Wales*, 1950

Norris, N. E. S. and Burstow, G. P. 'A Prehistoric and Romano-British Site at West Blatchington, Hove,' *Sussex Arch. Coll.* LXXXIX (1950), 1–56

Northumberland County History, Newcastle 1893–

Payne, F. G. 'The Plough in Ancient Britain,' *Arch.J.* CIV (1947), 82–111

Philips, J. T. 'Survey of the Distribution of Querns of Hunsbury or Allied Types,' *Trans. Leicester Arch. Soc.* XXVI (1950), 75–82

Piggott, Mrs C. M. 'The Excavations at Hownam Rings, Roxburghshire, 1948,' *PSAS* LXXXII (1947–8), 193–225
'The Iron Age Settlement at Hayhope Knowe, Roxburghshire: Excavations, 1949,' *PSAS* LXXXIII (1948–9), 63
'The Excavations at Bonchester Hill, 1950,' *PSAS* LXXXIV (1949–1950), 113–36

Piggott, Stuart 'Timber Circles: a Re-examination,' *Arch.J.* XCVI (1939), 193–222
British Prehistory, Oxford 1949
'Swords and Scabbards of the British Early Iron Age,' *PPS* XVI (1950), 1–28
'Excavations in the Broch and Hill-Fort of Torwoodlee, Selkirkshire 1950,' *PSAS* LXXXV (1950–1), 92–117
'Three Metal-work Hoards of the Roman Period from Southern Scotland,' *PSAS* LXXXVII (1952–3), 1–50
'The Archaeological Background,' in *The Problem of the Picts*, ed. F. T. Wainwright, Edinburgh 1955
'The Role of the City in Ancient Civilizations,' in *The Metropolis in Modern Life*, ed. R. M. Fisher, New York 1955

PPS *Proceedings of the Prehistoric Society*, new series, Cambridge

*PSAN*⁴ *Proceedings of the Society of the Antiquaries of Newcastle-upon-Tyne*, fourth series

PSAS *Proceedings of the Society of Antiquaries of Scotland*, Edinburgh

Radford, C. A. Ralegh 'The Tribes of Southern Britain,' *PPS* XX (1954), 1–26

Radford, C. A. R. and Donaldson, Gordon *Whithorn and Kirkmadrine, Wigtownshire*, Edinburgh 1953

Raistrick, A. 'Iron Age Settlements in West Yorkshire,' *YAJ* XXXIV (1938), 115–50

Raistrick, A. and Chapman, S. E. 'The Lynchet Groups of Upper Wharfedale, Yorkshire,' *Antiquity* III (1929), 165–81

Randall, H. J. 'Population and Agriculture in Roman Britain: a reply,' *Antiquity* IV (1930), 80–90

RCAM Royal Commission on Ancient Monuments:
East Lothian, Edinburgh 1924
Fife, Edinburgh 1933
Anglesey, 1937
Roxburghshire I, Edinburgh 1956

RCHM Royal Commission on Historic Monuments:
Westmorland, London 1936

Rhodes, P. P. 'The Celtic Field-Systems on the Berkshire Downs,' *Oxoniensia* (1950), 1–28

Richmond, I. A. 'Ptolemaic Scotland,' *PSAS* LVI (1921–2), 288–301
'Excavations on Hadrian's Wall in the Birdoswald–Pike Hill sector, 1929,' *CW*² XXX (1930), 169–205
'The Roman Fort at South Shields,' *AA*⁴ XI (1934), 81–102
'Excavations on the Estate of Meikleour, Perthshire 1939,' *PSAS* LXXIV (1939–40), 37–48
'Saint Cuthbert's Dwelling on Farne,' *Antiquity* XV (1941), 88–9
'Gnaeus Iulius Agricola,' *JRS* XXXIV (1944), 34–45
'The Four *Coloniae* of Roman Britain,' *Arch.J.* CIII (1946), 57–84
'The Sarmatae, *Bremetennacum Veteranorum* and the *Regio Bremetennacensis*,' *JRS* XXXV (1945), 15–29
'Excavations at the Roman Fort of Newstead, 1947,' *PSAS* LXXXIV (1949–50), 1–38
The Roman fort at South Shields: a guide, South Shields 1953
'Queen Cartimandua,' *JRS* XLIV (1954), 43–52

Richmond, I. A. and McIntyre, James 'The Roman Camps at Reycross and Crackenthorpe,' *CW*² XXXIV (1934), 50–61
'The Agricolan Fort at Fendoch,' *PSAS* LXXIII (1938–9), 110–54

Richmond, I. A. and Birley, E. 'Excavations at Corbridge, 1936–8,' *AA*⁴ XV (1938), 243–94
'Excavations at Corbridge, 1938–9,' *AA*⁴ XVII (1940), 85–115

Richmond, I. A. and Crawford, O. G. S. 'The British Section of the Ravenna Cosmography,' *Archaeologia* XCIII (1949), 1–50

Richmond, I. A. and Webster, G. 'Excavations in Goss Street, Chester, 1948–9,' *Chester Arch.J.* XXXVIII (1951), 1–38

Richmond, I. A. and St Joseph, J. K. and Gillam, J. P. 'The Roman Fort at Glenlochar, Kirkcudbrightshire,' *Trans. Dum. and Gall. Ant. & Nat. Hist. Soc.* XXX (1951–2), 1–16

Richmond, I. A. and Gillam, J. P. 'Buildings of the first and second

Centuries north of the granaries of Corbridge, *AA*[4] XXXI (1953), 205–53
'Excavations on the site of the Roman Fort at Lancaster 1950,' *Trans. of the Historic Society of Lancs. and Cheshire* CV (1953), 1–23
Ridgway, Sir William 'Niall "of the Nine Hostages" in connexion with the treasures of Traprain Law and Ballinrees and the destruction of Wroxeter, Chester, Caerleon and Caerwent,' *JRS* XIV (1924), 123–36
Robertson, Anne S. 'Roman Coins found in Scotland,' *PSAS* LXXXIV (1949–50), 137–69
Rowell, H. T. 'The Honesta Missio from the Numeri of the Roman Imperial Army,' *Yale Classical Studies* VI (1939), 73–108
Rylands, J. Glazebrook *The Geography of Ptolemy Elucidated*, Dublin 1893
St Joseph, J. K. 'Air Reconnaissance of North Britain,' *JRS* XLI (1951), 52–65
'The Avondale Road,' in *The Roman Occupation of SW. Scotland*, Glasgow 1952
'Air Reconnaissance of Southern Britain,' *JRS* XLIII (1953), 81–97
'Air Reconnaissance in Britain, 1951–5,' *JRS* XLV (1955), 82–91
Schleiermacher, W. 'Der obergermanische Limes und spätrömische Wehranlagen am Rhein,' *33 Bericht der römischen-germanischen Kommission*, 1943–50, 1951
Schnetz, J. (ed.) *Ravennatis Anonymi Cosmographia*, 2 vols, Leipzig (1939–40)
Scott, W. L. 'Corn-drying Kilns,' *Antiquity* XXV (1951), 196–208
Sellye, Ibolya 'Les Bronzes Émaillés de la Pannonie Romaine,' *Dissertationes Pannonicae*, ser. 2, fasc. 8, Budapest 1939
Shaw, R. C. 'Romano-British Carlisle: its Structural Remains,' *CW*[2] XXIV (1924), 95–109
Simpson, F. G. and Hodgson, K. S. 'The Coastal Mile-Fortlet at Cardurnock,' *CW*[2] XLVII (1947), 78–127
Smith, John 'Excavation of the Forts of Castlehill, Aitnock and Coalhill, Ayrshire,' *PSAS* LIII (1918–19), 123–34
Steer, K. A. and Keeney, G. S. 'Excavations in Two Homesteads at Crock Cleuch, Roxburghshire, *PSAS* LXXXI (1946–7), 138–57
Steer, K. A. and Feachem, R. W. 'The Roman Fort and Temporary Camp at Oakwood, Selkirkshire,' *PSAS* LXXXVI (1951–2), 81–105
Stevens, C. E. 'Gildas and the Civitates of Britain,' *EHR* LII (1937), 193–203
'The British Sections of the "Notitia Dignitatum,"' *Arch.J.* XCVII (1940), 123–54
'Gildas Sapiens,' *EHR* LVI (1941), 353–73
'Notes on Roman Chester,' *Chester Arch.J.* XXXV (1942), 49–52
'A possible conflict of Laws in Roman Britain,' *JRS* XXXVII (1947), 132–4
'Britain between the Invasions (54 B.C.–A.D. 43): A Study in Ancient Diplomacy,' in *Aspects of Archaeology in Britain and Beyond*, London 1951, 332–44
Varley, W. J. 'The Hill-Forts of the Welsh Marches,' *Arch.J.* CV (1948), 41–66

VCH *Victoria County Histories* : *Derbyshire* I, 1905

Wace, A. J. B. and Jehu, T. J. 'Cave Excavations in East Fife,' *PSAS* XLIX (1914–15), 233–55

Watson, W. J. *The History of the Celtic Place-Names of Scotland*, Edinburgh 1926

Wheeler, R. E. M. *Segontium and the Roman Occupation of Wales*, Cymrodorion Society, 1923

'The Roman town-walls of Arles,' *JRS* XVI (1926), 174–93

'Maiden Castle, Dorset.' *Reports of the Research Committee of the Society of Antiquaries of London* XII, London 1943

'The Stanwick Fortifications.' *Reports of the Research Committee of the Society of Antiquaries of London* XVII, London 1954

'The Stanwick Excavations, 1951. Interim Report,' *Ant.J.* XXXII (1952), 1–13

Wheeler, R. E. M. and Mrs Tessa Verney *Report on the Excavation of the Prehistoric, Roman and Post-Roman sites in Lydney Park, Gloucestershire*, Oxford 1932

Williams, A. 'The Excavations at Allard's Quarry, Marnhull, Dorset,' *Proc. Dorset Nat. Hist. & Arch. Soc.* LXXII (1950), 20–75

Worsfold, F. H. 'A Report on the Late Bronze Age Site excavated at Minnis Bay, Kent, 1938–40,' *PPS* IX (1943), 28–47

YAJ *Yorkshire Archaeological Journal*

INDEX

Printed in Great Britain by
Thomas Nelson and Sons Ltd, Edinburgh